Keys to Success
for Teaching Students
with Autism

Lori Ernsperger, Ph.D.
Autism Consultant
Henderson, NV

Keys to Success for Teaching Students with Autism

All marketing and publishing rights guaranteed to and reserved by

721 W. Abram Street
Arlington, Texas 76013
800-489-0727
817-277-0727
817-277-2270 (fax)
E-mail: info@futurehorizons-autism.com
www.FutureHorizons-autism.com

Cataloging in Publications Data is available from the Library of Congress.

ISBN   1-885477-92-9

In memory of Alecia Ellis

Whose tireless dedication and caring positively influenced

the lives of many children with autism and their families.

Acknowledgements

I have been fortunate to work with and learn from many talented and dedicated professionals. I feel particularly indebted to Dr. Ron Leaf and his staff at Autism Partnership. Ron has generously shared so much of his expertise in working with children with autism. I cannot adequately express my appreciation to a distinguished team of professionals to whom I had the honor to work with: Jan Butz, Nicki Compton, Susan D'Aniello, Jackie Green, Barb Webb, and Tammy White. In addition to their selfless dedication to the students they served, they are an outstanding group of women.

I would also like to thank Wayne Gilpin and the supportive staff at Future Horizons for making the commitment to publish this book. Their professionalism and dedication to this project is greatly appreciated.

This book would not have been completed without the support and endless encouragement from my family. To my mother and father, Anne and Fred Clark, whose values and determination I have cultivated from the seeds of excellence you planted in me as a child. Thank you to my children, Ben and Jessica, your kisses and hugs kept me strong over the years it took me to complete this book. And to my biggest fan, my husband, Tom, who has always supported my every endeavor.

Table of Contents

Introduction

Keys to Success for Teaching Students with Autism provides school personnel with a one-stop, practical guide for creating, designing, and implementing an effective educational program for students with autism and related disorders. Every year, more and more children are diagnosed with autism. This rapid increase not only creates an ever-greater demand for educators and other professionals to teach these students, it also creates a need for resources to help and guide both new and veteran teachers as they work with students with autism. To add to this dilemma, both new and veteran teachers often do not possess the specialized knowledge or the technical skills required to educate students with autism.

I have written this book to enable school personnel, regardless of their level of knowledge or training, create and implement an effective educational program for students with autism. This book is directed at practitioners and identifies and describes in a step-by-step approach the components necessary for designing and implementing an effective and efficient program.

To accomplish this, *Keys to Success for Teaching Students with Autism* has several objectives:

1. Provide educators with the history and knowledge of autism spectrum disorders.

2. Examine specific strategies for classroom design and scheduling.

3. Review instructional methods and step-by-step techniques for implementing these methods in the classroom.

4. Provide a variety of data collection forms and guidelines for implementation.

5. Examine basic strategies for developing an appropriate and functional curriculum.

6. Assist the multidisciplinary staff in conducting a functional assessment and writing a behavior intervention plan.

7. Identify proactive and reactive techniques for managing problem behaviors.

8. Enable licensed personnel and support staff to establish support networks and develop a collaborative team.

It is my intent to provide school personnel with the basic knowledge and requirements to successfully educate students with autism.

Overview of Autism Spectrum Disorders and PDD

The term autism means different things to different people. From its very definition to its causes and treatment, autism remains the "quintessential enigma" (Simpson & Miles, 1998).

Many people's perception of autism comes from the character of Raymond in the Oscar winning movie *Rainman;* to others autism includes those who are severely mentally retarded and extremely self-injurious. In reality, autistic behaviors lie somewhere between these two perceptions.

Part of the confusion surrounding autism is that it is not a single disorder, but a continuum of conditions with overlapping symptoms. Although researchers have studied autism for many years now, we still do not know exactly what causes it. Possible causes of autism cited by researchers are genetic factors, seizures, congenital rubella, and childhood vaccinations (Mesibov, Adams, & Klinger, 1997). Other studies have suggested that an imbalance in neurochemicals may cause autism (Anderson & Hoshino, 1997). We may not know the cause, but that doesn't reduce the need for teaching students with autism.

Three additional factors further complicate autism research:

- The tremendous increase in occurrence rates.

- The dramatic increase in the number of intervention approaches.

- An overall lack of trained personnel to serve the needs of people with autism.

The number of individuals diagnosed with pervasive developmental disorders, the broad category which includes autism, has increased dramatically over the past twenty years (Cohen & Volkmar, 1997). According to an earlier edition of the Diagnostic and Statistical Manual of Mental Disorders (3rd ed.; APA, 1980) between two and five children out of every 10,000 were identified as autistic. Recently, The Autism Society of America (ASA, 1999) quoted much higher rates of up to 20 in 10,000.

Several factors may have contributed to this increase in prevalence rates. First, experts now include autism in the broader range of pervasive developmental disorders (PDD) along with the milder autism subtypes such as Asperger's Syndrome and pervasive developmental disorders-not otherwise specified (Cohen & Volkmar, 1997).

Second, improved diagnostic tools have helped researchers identify persons with autism, many of whom would not have been diagnosed 20 years ago (Mesibov, Adams, & Klinger, 1997). Diagnosticians can now choose from a wide variety of tests to better identify children with both PDD and autism.

Finally, the increasing number of students with autism, coupled with the wide variety of intervention and treatment options has resulted in a greater demand for teachers specifically prepared to teach children with autism (Simpson, 1995). Part of this is due to a limited number of preservice special education programs which focus on autism (Simpson & Myles, 1998). Simpson (1995) found that, "anyone who has ever attempted to work with students with autism can attest to the need for specialized instructional and management skills and appropriate experiences" (p. 15).

We need teacher education programs that provide the skill development and field experience necessary to prepare prospective teachers to work in specialized fields (Goodlad, 1990). These programs are particularly important for teachers who are learning to teach students with autism.

Despite the need for autism-related training, and because of the emphasis on including students with autism in mainstream classes, there is a growing shift in the country towards generic teacher training. While good teaching and sound learning principles are very important in teaching students with autism, our new teachers are trained as generalists in the special education field. This certainly has many benefits, but there is still a need for specialists who are trained extensively in teaching students with autism.

Historical Background of Autism

The history of autism in the United States is relatively brief when compared to other disabilities. Autism was first described in 1943 when Dr. Leo Kanner, a psychiatrist at Johns Hopkins University, published a paper entitled "Autistic Disturbances of Affective Contact" (Kanner, 1943). In that paper, Dr. Kanner described 11 children with three common characteristics which were different from other children he had studied:

- Social isolation

- Insistence on sameness

- Abnormal language

This "triad of behaviors" as it is called is the primary criteria in the diagnosis of autism (Wing, 1981).

While Dr. Kanner was researching infantile autism in the 1940s, the German physician Hans Asperger was working with a group of children who, like those observed by Kanner, had severe difficulties in social integration. Unlike Dr. Kanner's children, however, Dr. Asperger's children had average verbal and cognitive abilities (Myles & Simpson, 1998).

Asperger's children, to be sure, had idiosyncratic verbal communication, social integration problems, and were physically clumsy (Klin & Volkmar, 1997; Frith, 1989). But they were also highly verbal and appeared to have no cognitive disabilities. Obviously this group of children, while they shared some symptoms, were different from those children identified by Kanner. Due to a lack of English translation, Hans Asperger's work was not available in the United States until recently (Myles & Simpson, 1998).

During the early 1950s and 1960s, researchers attempted to understand the causes of autism within the psychoanalytic field. For example, Kanner originally believed that infantile autism was caused by problems within the family (Mesibov, Adams, & Klinger, 1997). He suggested that emotional conflicts and inadequate parenting caused autism (Mesibov, Adams, & Klinger, 1997; Siegel, 1997).

Another major force behind parental blaming was the work of Bruno Bettelheim. Bettelheim believed parents caused autism by their behavior toward their children. In 1967, Bettelheim published his book *The Empty Fortress* in which he theorized that autism is a reaction to emotional deprivation from non-nurturing parents (Bettelheim, 1967). Mothers in particular were blamed for their children's disorder, and were labeled "refrigerator mothers". According to Cohen and Volkmar (1997), Bettelheim's opinion, as well as its popularity, "is a black mark on the history of autism" (p. 949).

The basic assumptions of the psychoanalytic theory were finally called into question during the 1970s when epidemiological data refuted claims that autism was caused by any family or emotional factors. Studies demonstrated that autism is found in families in which positive parental interaction and intensity of interactions are no different than in normal developing children (Scott, Clark, & Brady, 2000).

Another study reviewed personality profiles of mothers with autistic children and found no personality traits such as neuroticism or other psychiatric disorders (Mesibov, Adams, & Klinger, 1997). The accumulating evidence against the psychoanalytic theory of autism finally led researchers to look towards a possible biological or neurological cause of autism rather than an emotional cause. The blame on mothers decreased and researchers began to investigate other contributing factors.

Epidemiological studies have increased over the last two decades. Current research includes the study of brain development and functioning, theories of cognitive and social development, genetic research, and the effects of prenatal complications (Cohen & Volkmar, 1997; Frith, 1989; Rodier, 2000; Tsai, 1999). Other studies have examined a variety of neurochemicals such as serotonin and dopamine, both of which have been strongly suspected of causing autism (Koegel & Koegel, 1995; Mesibov, Adams, & Klinger, 1997; Tsai, 1999). It is clear that autism is not caused by psychological or family factors. But the true cause of autism remains a mystery.

Diagnostic Criteria and Classification

While researchers sought the causes of autism during the late 1960s and 1970s clinicians and researchers were working on the more practical task of attempting to appropriately diagnose and classify individuals with autism. They were using early editions of the American Psychiatric Association's (APA) Diagnostic and Statistical Manual of Mental Disorders (DSM), a manual which describes the symptoms and diagnostic criteria for identifying and diagnosing mental disorders. These early versions did not list autism separately. They listed only childhood schizophrenia to describe and classify children with autism (Mesibov, Adams, & Klinger, 1997). Because of the lack of a specific entry for autism and related disorders, children with autism were also labeled with symbiotic psychosis, severe emotional disturbance, or mental retardation (Freeman, 1997).

Finally, in 1980, the definition of autism, formulated by the Autism Society of America (ASA), was introduced to the DSM-III. The DSM-III included the description of autism, along with several other disorders, under a new category of Pervasive Developmental Disorders (PDD). The two subtypes for PDD were residual infantile autism and childhood onset pervasive developmental disorder (Volkmar, Klin, & Cohen, 1997).

Shortly after the publication of the DSM-III in 1980, researchers made significant advances in the classification of autism and other developmental disorders (Mesibov, Adams, & Klinger, 1997). The first change to the DSM-III included the dropping of the thirty-month minimum age requirement for early onset. This change allowed clinicians to make a diagnosis based on current examinations regardless of the child's history.

The second major change was in the subtype categories. "Infantile autism" was changed to "autism disorder" to reflect the persistence of this condition throughout the life span. "Childhood Onset Pervasive Developmental Disorder" was dropped and replaced with "Pervasive Developmental Disorder-Not Otherwise Specified" (PDD-NOS). The final major change to the DSM-III was the addition of the "triad of behaviors", first identified by Dr. Kanner, to diagnose an individual with autism:

- Qualitative impairment in reciprocal social interaction.

- Qualitative impairment in verbal and nonverbal communication and in imagination.

- Restricted repertoire of activities and interests.

After further revisions and a national field trial, the definitions in the DSM-III-R (revised) were accepted by the American Psychiatric Association in 1987.

While the American Psychiatric Association made revisions to the DSM-III-R, the World Health Organization (WHO) was revising its equivalent, the International Classification of Diseases (ICD).

There were several disparities between the DSM-III-R and the ICD. For example, Asperger's Disorder, Rett's disorder, and childhood disintegrative disorder were included in the ICD, but were not in the DSM-III-R. After field trials and a review of the literature, the fourth edition of the DSM, the DSM IV, was published in 1994. It included the

subtypes identified earlier by the ICD. The DSM-IV is still the most current authority on

autism and its related disorders. (For a thorough review of the current diagnostic criteria

in the DSM-IV see Appendix B.

In 1990, the U.S. Congress passed the Individuals with Disabilities Education Act, or

IDEA as it is commonly known. Although the Education for All Handicapped Act (EHA)

had been in effect since 1975, it did not include autism as a separate disability category.

The enactment of IDEA resolved that shortcoming, defining autism as:

> *A developmental disability significantly affecting verbal and nonverbal*
>
> *communication and social interaction, generally evident before the age three, that*
>
> *adversely affects educational performance. Characteristics of autism include—*
>
> *irregularities and impairment in communication, engagement in repetitive*
>
> *activities and stereotyped movements, resistance to environmental change or*
>
> *change in daily routines, and unusual responses to sensory experiences.*

Not included in IDEA were separate categories for each subtype such as Asperger's

syndrome, Rett's disorder, or childhood disintegrative disorder.

In close collaboration with medical personnel, educators use the diagnostic criteria in

the DSM-IV to establish a student's eligibility for specialized education and training under

IDEA. This collaboration is critical for ensuring that students with autism receive an

appropriate diagnosis and subsequent therapy and training. (In some states a medical diagnosis of autistic disorder must be confirmed by a licensed physician or clinical psychologist before a multidisciplinary team can determine an educational eligibility of autism.)

Subtypes of Pervasive Developmental Disorders

The DSM-IV lists five subcategories of pervasive developmental disorders:

1. Autistic disorder

2. Childhood disintegrative disorder

3. Rett's disorder

4. Asperger's syndrome

5. Pervasive developmental disorder-not otherwise specified(PDD-NOS)

While specific diagnostic criteria for each subtype can be reviewed in the appendices, an overview is provided here to clarify the distinctions between each category and provide the reader with a working definition of each disorder.

1. Autistic Disorder

Autistic Disorder is by far the most common diagnosis found under PDD. Autism is a spectrum of characteristics that range from significant cognitive and verbal impairment to those individuals who are extremely high functioning and verbal. According to the ASA (1999),

"Autism is a severely incapacitating life-long developmental disability that typically appears during the first three years of life. The result of a neurological disorder that affects functioning of the brain, autism and its behavioral symptoms occur approximately twenty out of every 10,000 births."

The ASA goes on to say that, "autism is four times more likely in boys than girls. It has also been found throughout the world in families of all racial, ethnic, and social backgrounds."

Most individuals who are diagnosed with autistic disorder are considered to have moderate to severe cognitive disabilities, and about three-fourths of individuals with autistic disorder are considered to be mentally retarded.

While those numbers may appear discouraging, we must remember that there are many people with autism who can and do excel, even when compared with neurotypical people.

One such person is Temple Grandin, an assistant professor of animal science at Colorado State University. She holds a doctorate in animal husbandry and is a high-functioning person with autism.

Dr. Grandin wrote about her experiences with autism in her 1996 book, *Emergence: Labeled Autistic.* Excerpts from her book about some of her childhood experiences are used here to illustrate the triad of behaviors which characterize individuals with autism.

Difficulty with social interaction is one of the most noticeable characteristics of people with autism. In social situations they avoid eye contact, lack facial expression, and use unusual body gestures. This combination of behaviors makes children with autism appear neutral or "flat". These children may also lack empathy, making it difficult for them to develop personal relationships. The result is a person who is, at best, excluded from normal peer relationships, and at worst is bullied and harassed by both teachers and other students.

Temple Grandin's words graphically illustrate this difficulty. She remembers "…being bombarded with negative impressions. A sense of isolation envelops me. I am overwhelmed with remembrances of noisy hallways jammed with students and cruel peer rejection and teachers' negative attitudes."

Along with social integration difficulties, individuals with autism may also have difficulty communicating. These difficulties range from the inability to develop any functional speech to the development of understandable but idiosyncratic language. Even if the child is able to speak, he or she may lack the ability to hold a conversation. Individuals with autism may also have trouble with conversational skills such as voice intonation, pitch, fluency and speech rate.

Dr. Grandin describes her attempts at communicating with others as "a continuing problem. I often sounded abrasive and abrupt. In my head I knew what I wanted to say but the words never matched my thoughts. I was also not aware of my persistence or hesitation and (the) occasional flat tone of my speech".

Persons with autism may also have other language abnormalities such as pronoun reversal or echolalia. Echolalia is the rote repetition of the exact words heard. For children with autism, echolalia may occur immediately, that is, the child may repeat something he just heard, or it may be delayed, and the child will repeat a word or phrase—or even an entire commercial heard days earlier. Some researchers believe echolalia serves a purpose by signifying that the child wants to communicate but doesn't know what to say or how to say it. There is even some indication that echolalic responses can be used to develop true spontaneous speech.

The last criteria in the triad of behaviors used to identify individuals with autism is "repetitive and restricted stereotypical patterns of activities and interests". The child with autism may have a preoccupation with a particular item—a toy or other object—or she may have other interests that are very restricted (Scott, Clark, & Brady, 2000). She may also exhibit inflexible adherence to routines, refusing to change even for logical reasons, and becomes very emotional when forced to change.

Dr. Temple Grandin (1996) explains her need for routines: "Like most autistics I wanted everything the same. I even wore the same jacket and dressed in the same kind of clothes day in and day out".

Another form of repetitive activity is self-stimulation such as rocking, hand flapping, spinning, and other rhythmic motor movements which provide pleasurable stimulation. This self-stimulating behavior, along with other unusual repetitive behavior, is often a barrier to both social acceptance and social integration of individuals with autism.

Apart from the triad of symptoms, children with autism experience a variety of other problems including sleep difficulties, self-injurious behavior, eating disorders, and motor coordination problems. Individuals with autistic disorder are often either over-sensitive to auditory or tactile stimulation, or they do not react to them at all. Since the characteristics of autism are on a continuum from mild to severe, each child with autism is different, making the student with autism at once similar to, and very different from, the ordinary student.

2. Childhood Disintegrative Disorder

In the early 1900's Theodore Heller described a group of children who, after an early period of normal development, began to regress developmentally. It wasn't until 1987, however, that the World Health Organization included what is now known as childhood disintegrative disorder (CDD) as a separate category in the International Classification of Diseases (ICD). This disorder differs from autism in that the child develops normally for at least two years, and then begins to regress in his development. The behavioral and clinical features of CDD resemble autism: social skills are markedly impaired, communication skills are limited, and unusual stereotyped patterns of behavior are present. Autistic disorder and CDD are very similar, so a review of the child's history is critical before the child is diagnosed with CDD.

Childhood disintegrative disorder is relatively rare and much less common than other PDD. The available prevalence data for CDD are unreliable because clinicians are unfamiliar with this type of developmental disorder. Prognosis and outcomes for individuals with CDD appear to be similar to those with autistic disorder, and the DSM-IV notes that the "social, communicative, and behavioral difficulties [of CDD] remain constant throughout life".

3. Rett's Disorder

In 1966 Andreas Rett, an Austrian physician, published a report describing twenty-two girls who exhibited unusual hand movements, dementia, lack of physical coordination, autistic-like behavior, and deterioration of parts of the brain. Rett's Disorder was eventually included in the DSM-IV as one of the five subcategories under PDD. According to the APA, Rett's Disorder occurs exclusively in females between one and two years old. These children usually develop in an apparently normal fashion during the first five months of life (Scott, Clark, & Brady, 2000). Behavioral characteristics of this disability include excessive hand patting, waving and other involuntary movements. Other symptoms include slowed head growth, poor motor coordination, and severe impairment of receptive and expressive skills.

Rett's Disorder occurs in about one of every 22,800 female births, although the identification rate is low because physicians and educators usually don't recognize Rett's syndrome. Most experts believe the disorder lasts a lifetime.

4. Asperger's Syndrome

In 1944 Dr. Hans Asperger, an Austrian psychiatrist, first described the syndrome that bears his name. Only in the last twenty years, however, has Asperger's syndrome been recognized and regularly diagnosed.

The diagnostic criteria for Asperger's syndrome outlined in the DSM-IV include impaired communication skills, social skills deficits, and narrow interests. Children with Asperger's syndrome do not appear to have significant delays in language development; by the age of five, a child with Asperger's syndrome speaks fluently but with some limitations.

The social skill deficits of Asperger's children may include a lack of empathy, difficulty forming friendships, and trouble adjusting to change. These children may appear emotionally aloof and insensitive to others, but are actually hypersensitive to relationships and are frustrated by their inability to engage in meaningful and appropriate relationships.

Children with Asperger's syndrome may exhibit very narrow interests. Such as memorizing birthdays, collecting trains, studying snakes, or any of a thousand special interests. Regardless of the chosen interest, it often dominates the child's activities, and as the child gets older, the special interests typically become more unusual and narrow in focus. Their intense study of and interest in their particular special interest, coupled with their social ineptness, often causes children with Asperger's syndrome to be shunned by their peers and suffer from low self-esteem (Cohen & Volkmar, 1997).

Keys to Success for Teaching Students with Autism

Because of the difficulty in diagnosing Asperger's syndrome, many people are not diagnosed until later in life, some as late as there forties. While this is unusual, it demonstrates the subjective nature of the diagnostic criteria.

5. Pervasive Developmental Disorder-Not Otherwise Specified

The fifth subtype of PDD identified in the DSM-IV is pervasive developmental disorder-not otherwise specified (PDD-NOS). The diagnostic guidelines for PPD-NOS are ambiguous, so all other disorders must be ruled out before a person can be included in this category. According to the DSM-IV (APA, 1994), children identified with PDD-NOS do not meet the criteria for other pervasive developmental disorders. Individuals diagnosed with PDD-NOS may be considered to have mild autism (Towbin, 1997). Broader definitions and improved assessment methods are increasing the number of individuals identified with PDD-NOS, but until specific criteria are applied to this population, we don't know how many people have this disorder.

Prevalence

Recent estimates of the occurrence of all pervasive development disorders have been as high as 15 to 20 out of every 10,000. Notably, an estimated occurrence rate of ten out of every ten thousand is higher than the frequency for childhood cancer, diabetes or Down syndrome.

Whatever the actual prevalence rate, the increase is very real and the reasons are not completely clear. One explanation may be that current studies of occurrence rates include a broader definition of PDD. Another factor may be an increasing awareness among parents and professionals of the disorder. Moreover, a better understanding of diagnostic instruments and assessment techniques have influenced the occurrence rate for autism.

Assessment and Evaluation

For every child with a developmental delay, a unique series of thoughtful and comprehensive assessments is required so that both school personnel and parents can determine how best to teach that child. A "prescriptive assessment" is a process of collecting data to identify the child's strengths and weaknesses, formulate a diagnosis, and develop an agenda for future program planning (Simpson & Myles, 1998).

According to the Handbook of Autism and Pervasive Developmental Disorders (Cohen & Volkmar, 1997), the following guidelines should be used by the evaluation team in the assessment of a child with possible developmental delays:

1. Assess multiple areas of functioning.

2. Adopt a developmental perspective.

3. Identify specific skills and variable skills.

4. Review variability across settings.

5. Assess functional and adaptive skills.

6. Identify delays and deviance from normal development.

The evaluation team should include educators, psychologists, social workers, speech and language clinicians, audiologists, medical personnel, and, of course, parents. Each member of the evaluation team should possess a general understanding of autism, as well as the basic tools required for a comprehensive diagnostic assessment. For example, participants in an educational evaluation should be familiar with the characteristics, patterns, and stereotypical behaviors associated with autism.

I want to emphasize here that parental involvement is a critical component to a successful evaluation. Parents should be the primary source of information about a young child's development and behavior. Sharing information among professionals and parents demystifies evaluation procedures and helps parents better understand the child's disability.

A comprehensive evaluation, based on the particular needs of each child, should consist of several tests. Traditional psychological evaluations may include:

- A standardized measurement for testing intelligence,

- A measurement of achievement, and

- Tests of adaptive behavior and social skills.

The evaluation team, including the parents, should consider the extent of testing based on the individual age of the child, level of verbal communication, and other practical considerations.

In addition to the standardized tests traditionally used in an evaluation, a disability-specific assessment, including interviews and direct observations, should be a principal component of any assessment program. There are several diagnostic instruments which have been developed to evaluate children suspected of autism. The following are examples of diagnostic tools developed for determining eligibility of autism:

1. Childhood Autism Rating Scale (CARS) (Schopler, Reichler, & Renner, 1988) is a behavior rating scale which can be completed by the child's teacher, parent or therapist. The child's behavior is rated in fifteen different areas. The rating scale can be completed by a variety of different individuals who are familiar with the child.

2. Gilliam Autism Rating Scale (GARS) (Gilliam, 1995) is designed for use with individuals ages three through twenty-two, with test items based on the criteria from the DSM-IV. The GARS is fairly easy and quick to administer. The items are grouped according to stereotypical behaviors, communication and language development, and social interactions.

3. Autism Diagnostic Observation Schedule (ADOS) (Lord, Rutter, Goode, Heemsbergen, Goode, Mawhood, & Schopler, 1989) is a standardized protocol for the observation of communicative and social behaviors which are associated with autism. The examiner administers eight different tasks designed to assess the child's skills in turn-taking, symbolic play, and nonverbal and conversational language. The ADOS is most effective for

children above the age of four, and when supplemented by a parent interview.

4. Autism Diagnostic Interview-Revised (ADI-R) Lord, Rutter, & Le Couteur, 1994) is a semi-structured, standardized diagnostic interview that includes questions relevant to past and current functioning of preschool children who have been referred for possible autism. The revised interview is appropriate for children from eighteen months to adulthood. The questions focus on the caregivers descriptions of actual behavior. The results are aligned with the diagnostic criteria found in the ICD (International Classification of Diseases) and DSM-IV.

5. Parent Interview for Autism (PIA) (Stone & Hogan, 1993) is a structured interview developed to gather information from parents with children under six years of age. Parents are asked to make judgments about the frequency of behaviors indicative of autism.

A comprehensive assessment completed by a multidisciplinary team should establish eligibility, provide a reliable baseline of strengths and weaknesses, and identify goals and objectives for educational programming (Scott, Clark, & Brady, 2000).

Chapter One
Creating a Positive Environment

An effective educational program for students with autism, like any effective education program, is based on the creation of a positive classroom environment. An effective environment addresses the student's social, communication, and behavioral needs in a surrounding that is both supportive and encouraging. Moreover, it allows the student to learn and understand the patterns and rules of the classroom and school.

Chapter One will address the following objectives, so the reader should be able to:

- Design an effective classroom.

- Identify a variety of thematic units and age appropriate materials.

- Design work centers to meet student needs in each domain area.

- Identify strategies for creating a data collection center.

- Provide techniques for addressing environmental stimuli outside of the classroom.

- Assist school personnel in developing a variety of classroom and individual schedules.

- Support teachers, paraprofessionals, and related service personnel in creating a collaborative work environment.

The educational environment consists of the physical layout of the classroom as well as the schedules and staff responsibilities. A positive classroom environment sets the tone for student learning and helps students succeed. Students are able to increase learning and transition from activities with an appropriate classroom design and schedule while minimizing behavioral problems. The following guidelines should be reviewed and implemented throughout the school year. Teachers should consider each guideline to insure each has been thoroughly addressed.

A classroom inventory has been developed to assist teachers and staff in creating a positive classroom environment. The classroom inventory is designed for all settings including early childhood, elementary, and secondary classrooms. Students at all ages require similar environmental controls and adaptations. Professional judgement is required to insure the age appropriateness of each guideline. A sample classroom inventory is included in Appendix A.

CLASSROOM ENVIRONMENT

Helpful Hint: Classroom Inventory

Schedule a time to complete the classroom inventory with another trusted professional. Consider walking through the classroom with a paraprofessional or related service personnel. Discuss each guideline and determine if it is being met and what action may need to be taken.

Ensure the physical layout of the classroom is maximized and workstations clearly delineated.

It is important to provide a physical structure that supports learning and reduces distractions for both students and staff. Classrooms for students with autism are often too small and badly designed to meet those students' needs. A well designed classroom and clearly defined work stations provide visual cues for students to increase independence.

If classroom size is small, be sure to reduce clutter and organize materials and resources for accessibility and safety. Remember, students with autism have difficulty filtering out distracting visual and auditory stimuli, so it is important to create an environment that reduces distractions and allows the students to focus on learning.

Steps for Implementation:

- Label each workstation or learning center with large signs. Consider hanging a laminated picture label from the ceiling to designate each work area.

- Use desks, shelves, and filing cabinets to partition off specific areas. Furniture should be perpendicular to the wall to create well-defined work centers.

- Remove unwanted materials and furniture. Review each item in the classroom to be sure it important and useful.

- Use colored tape to establish boundaries. Tape can be easily applied to the floor and removed as necessary. If tape is not practical, colored chalk can be used to create boundaries, although it must be reapplied frequently.

- Determine appropriate activities for each learning center. For example, a center with a tile floor is more appropriate for snack time than for language arts.

 Helpful Hint: "Throw it Away"

The first step in getting organized is reducing the clutter in your classroom. Don't be a pack rat! If you think you may need that large box you used last year as a planetarium, ask the custodian for a place in the building to store it. Custodians know every nook and cranny in the building and if shown some consideration, they may be able to assist you.

Ensure work stations or learning centers are designed to support group instruction, individual instruction, and transition periods.

Students with autism are often very active and require support when transitioning around the classroom. The physical layout of the classroom should be carefully designed to minimize open spaces and reduce "run ways." The traffic flow of students and staff should decrease waiting time and meet the needs of individual students. Furniture arrangement should support both small and large group instruction and facilitate smooth transitions.

Steps to Implementation:

- Design classroom layout according to class schedule.

- Designate specific areas for small group or one-on-one instruction.

- Provide opportunities for students to learn the schedule.

- Furniture should be an appropriate size for the age of the student.

- Use an auditory cue such as a kitchen timer or song to indicate transition periods.

- Use colored feet or traffic arrows to designate traffic flow from each learning center.

Materials should be organized, clean, and work properly.

All materials must be in good working order and ready to use in order to maximize every learning opportunity and maintain student engagement. Students with autism often require tangible materials and reinforcement to learn new skills. Therefore, all staff and students must keep components together and maintain the quality of classroom materials. Keeping materials organized will save valuable time for staff and students.

Steps to Implementation:

- Purchase extra batteries for materials.

- Assign a staff person to check materials daily.

- Rotate the cleaning of materials. For example, Monday wash all materials in the Sensory Center; Tuesday check and wash materials in the Play and Fine Motor Center, etc.

- Purchase duplicates of favorite games and tangible reinforcers.

- Label shelves and cabinets with both a picture of the item and the corresponding written word.

- Teach students to return materials to their proper location.

Classroom décor and materials are linked to thematic units.

Thematic instruction is an organizational tool where specific units are developed and learning objectives are implemented across the content areas. Thematic instruction increases the relevance of the curriculum and allows for repetitive teaching opportunities across life domains such as play and leisure skills, academics, and communication. It also facilitates generalization of newly acquired skills and increases learning opportunities. Thematic instruction has been effectively used at the elementary level, but it can also be used effectively with secondary school students. Therefore the classroom curriculum and décor should be based on a thematic unit.

Steps for Implementation:

- Recruit other staff members in planning and selecting themes for the school year.

- Identify age appropriate themes.

- Use each unit for four to six weeks.

- Create bulletin boards and teaching materials which are linked to the thematic unit.

- Ask other teachers for ideas and share materials.

- Organize an afternoon "Make and Take Workshop" with a group of teachers. Create materials for an entire month.

Classroom environment and learning centers facilitate instruction across all life domains

The classroom structure, workstations, and schedules must facilitate learning across life domains. They must also address social and communication disabilities. Students with autism spectrum disorders may have deficits or splinter skills in each life domain, and the classroom structure and schedule must address these as well. Please see Chapter 2 for a detailed explanation of Life Domains. Identify workstations and one-on-one areas for each of these life domain applications:

- Speech/Language
- Social/Emotional

- Self-help
- Gross Motor

- Play/leisure
- Fine Motor

- Sensory
- Cognitive/Academic

Unfortunately classrooms are too often designed to facilitate learning in the cognitive and academic areas and neglect opportunities in the other life domains. As we review the physical layout of an effective classroom, consider how each life domain is equally supported throughout the classroom.

Key Concept: Life Domains

Teaching essential skills across all life domains applies to students of all ages. Secondary students have similar needs in play, sensory, and fine and gross motor skills. A Life Domain Matrix is included in Appendix C. Walk through the classroom and complete the Life Domain Matrix. Be sure that each domain is addressed in the schedule.

Designated workstation can serve dual purposes, too. For example, the snack area may also be used for sensory and speech/language acquisition.

Steps to Implementation:

- Designate and label each station according to the life domains. A laminated poster taped to a table can clearly state the activities for that area.

- Use work stations for more than one life domain.

- Determine which life domains are not being addressed and develop appropriate activities to be included in the schedule.

Create an area designed for quiet or break time.

All students experience some level of stress and need time to relax, calm down, and reduce frustration. Students with autism are no different. Students with ASD must also learn twice as much as their neurotypical peers; while a normally developing student is focusing solely on academics, the student with autism is also learning new social skills and social rules. Therefore, it is important to give them a break area in the classroom. A designated area where they can relieve stress and calm themselves.

Please note that this is not considered a time-out or punitive area. The use of time-out for students with autism will be discussed in Chapter Four.

Steps to Implementation:

- Select an area free of distractions.

- Provide comfortable seating and relaxing materials. (i.e. books and stress release balls).

- The occupational therapist can provide some relaxation methods for the students to use in the break area.

- Once the student is calm, use the break area to teach stress reduction techniques.

Ensure the teacher's desk, teaching resources, and data collection materials are properly in place.

After creating a positive classroom environment and meeting the individual needs of students, the teacher must also provide an area for the staff to store their personal belongings, stockpile resource materials, and provide for data collection.

Steps for Implementation:

- Reduce the number of teacher's desks in the classroom. Teacher desks are sometimes large and bulky and take up too much space, so it may not be feasible for every staff member to have a desk.

- Maintain personal belongings in a locked cabinet or cupboard.

- Place unused teaching items in locked cupboards to reduce distractions for students.

- Maintain computer equipment in a secured location. Students may unwillingly damage computers that are left unattended.

- Purchase small luggage locks to secure cupboards and cabinets.

 Helpful Hint: Create A Data Collection Center

Data collection is a continuous process, so it is essential to have a data collection area that is accessible and usable by all staff members. Create file folders or clipboards that can be hung on the wall or placed easily on a shelf. Clear plastic mailboxes attached to the wall can be used for frequently accessed materials. Specific data collection methods will be discussed in Chapter Five.

Give careful consideration to lighting, windows, floor coverings and ceilings.

Sensory issues are very important to children with autism. Light, sound, and smell influences that are minor for normal children can be major distractions to a child with autism. Therefore the classroom should be as "sensory sensitive" as possible.

Much of the structure of a classroom can't be changed. Still, the staff must do what it can to reduce distractions caused by floors, ceilings, lights, and windows in the classroom. Some modifications can be easily made. Lowering shades and turning down overhead lights, for example, may reduce distractions for some students.

While the goal is to teach students the skills required to maintain on task behaviors in spite of outside distractions, some modifications can still be made.

Steps for Implementation:

- Use carpets to reduce noise levels.

- Small carpet squares may be used for seating arrangements.

- Tile flooring or plastic drop cloths can be used to protect carpeting.

- Use miniblinds or curtains on windows.

- Face desks or work stations away from windows.

- Check lighting for faulty bulbs.

Ensure doorways and safety standards are implemented.

For some students with autism, running out of the classroom has been reinforced to the point where it has become a serious safety concern. As with any maladaptive behavior, the teacher's goal is to provide students with the necessary skills to avoid running. A few small environmental changes can be implemented to reduce running. Security measures should also be reviewed to insure safety outside of the classroom and on the playground.

Steps for Implementation:

- Arrange furniture to reduce open spaces.

- Without blocking emergency exits or other doorways, strategically place a physical barrier close to the exits.

- Attach a small bell to the top of the door to alert staff.

- Place a large red STOP sign on the door and heavily reinforce the student for stopping.

- Assign one staff member to watch students who run or wander away from the group.

- Develop a quick safety plan in case a student leaves school property.

Create a positive school environment
beyond the special education classroom.

Teachers can use a number of strategies to support individual students within the classroom. The task of designing and implementing supports outside the classroom, however, is much more challenging. The entire staff must thoroughly and carefully review all areas of the campus to insure student safety. Particular areas of concern are the playground, cafeteria, gymnasium, library, and art rooms. Where possible, modifications to these areas should be considered.

Steps for Implementation:

- Educate and train the entire staff on the needs of each of the students in your classroom. Send student profiles to each classroom teacher who will come into contact with the students.

- Meet frequently with school administrators.

- Take the class on a tour of the kitchen when there are no other students in the cafeteria. Meet the cafeteria staff. Practice going through the line and designate one table for the class to sit at each day. Label and mark that table with a laminated visual cue outlining the rules for the cafeteria.

- Consider best practices for including students in mainstream classrooms. Some students with autism would be better included during a structured teaching time and not during Art/Music/PE.

- Send Reinforcement Buckets. (See Chapter Four)

- Provide visual supports and schedules before, during, and after the students leave the classroom. Remember, as the structure of the environment decreases, the number of visual supports must increase.

Conclusion

School personnel rarely have the opportunity to create the perfect classroom. Often, classroom selection for special education rooms are determined by space availability and the needs of the general education classrooms. Whenever possible enlist the help of school administrators in selecting an appropriate classroom.

Review the Classroom Inventory and determine which guidelines can be easily implemented. Develop an action plan for those more difficult guidelines. Remember that designing and structuring a classroom is a continuous process. During the school year the physical layout of the classroom must change to meet the changing needs of the students. Further, the student population changes throughout the year, with students moving in and out of the classroom. Be careful that the needs of both old and new students are met.

Key Concept: Minimizing Problem Behaviors

Problem behaviors can often be reduced or eliminated by creating an appropriate classroom environment. Environmental modifications can reduce student frustration and relieve stress.

Although students with autism prefer sameness and a rigid structure, it is important not to overly support their rigidness. Changes must constantly be made in both the classroom and in the schedule to help students learn coping skills. Small changes in seating arrangements or minor changes to the schedule will provide opportunities to teach frustration tolerance and stress management skills.

Sample Floor Plan

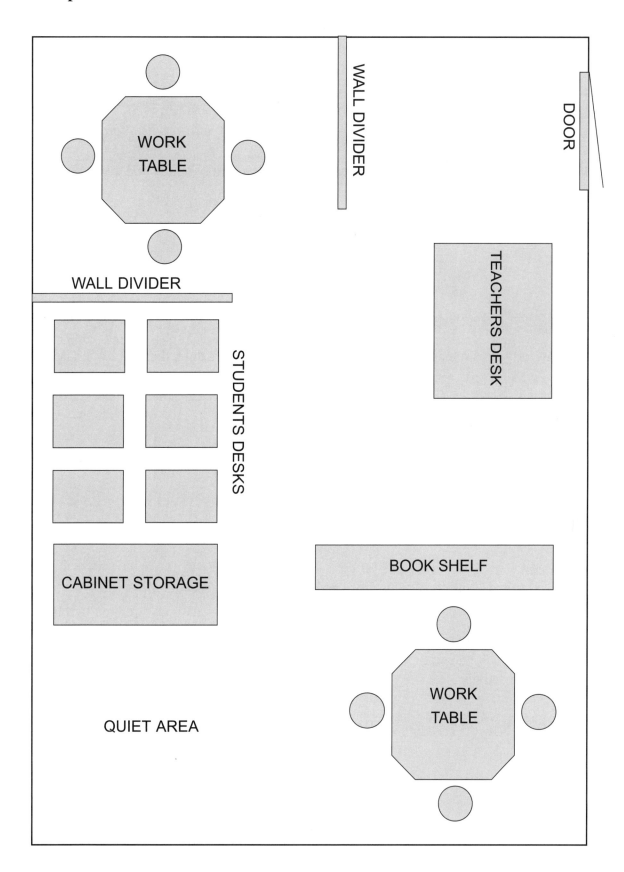

CLASSROOM SCHEDULES

A schedule is one key element for teaching students with autism. A well-organized and precise schedule provides the basis for a smooth running classroom and reduces problem behaviors. Effective classrooms for students with autism will often use two or three schedules simultaneously, including a daily classroom schedule and a schedule for each individual student.

The Daily Classroom Schedule

The first schedule is an overall schedule for the classroom. Since the behavior of students with autism may be disrupted by changes in the schedule, the staff can assist the student with a written and visual schedule. The daily classroom schedule is designed to provide predictability and a routine for all students.

Guidelines for the Classroom Schedule:

- Include the time and the specific activity.

- Provide both the written word and a picture on the schedule.

- The picture may be a representation of the activity or an actual photograph of the activity.

- Review the schedule with all students at the beginning of the day.

• During the daily review, particular attention is paid to any changes in the schedule. If the staff knows of any upcoming changes in the schedule, this should be brought   to the attention of the students with a visual cue.

• Create a schedule that allows sufficient time for transitions and changes in routines.

• To decrease problem behaviors at the beginning of the year, it may be necessary to initially provide a schedule in which the students remain in one workstation or learning center while the staff rotates to the student.

The following is an example of a daily schedule for a primary elementary classroom:

8:00-8:15

Student Arrival

8:15-9:00

Morning Circle

9:00-9:15

Restroom

9:15-10:00

Individual Work Centers

10:00-10:15

Computer

10:15-10:30

Recess

10:30-11:15

Individual Work Centers

11:15-11:30

Music

11:30-12:15

Lunch

10 Easy Steps for Creating a Classroom Schedule

1. Identify specific activities across the life domains. Be sure to include social and play skills.

2. Consider a developmentally appropriate length of time for each activity or workstation.

3. Create a schedule that reflects both sedentary and active learning times.

4. Eliminate or minimize "free play" or down time. Even during break time, students should be working on skills for stress management.

5. Use a computer to print out pictures to coordinate with each activity. A camera may be used to capture the activity for later viewing.

6. Add the written word to each activity.

7. Laminate each picture and use Velcro® to attach it to the schedule.

8. Develop a large file folder to store unused pictures.

9. Post the schedule at student eye level.

10. Review the schedule with all students at the beginning of the day.

The Individual Student Schedule

The second type of schedule is designed to meet the individual needs of students. In order for some students to maximize their learning, it may be necessary to develop an individualized schedule that lets them know where they are going throughout the day. The individual student schedule is designed to be portable. It should contain a variety of activities to keep the student motivated and engaged. The schedule should be well rounded and balanced with opportunities for small group, large group and direct instruction, as well as for independent work.

Again, use Velcro® to attach pictures and labels to a folder, cardboard, or a clipboard to be carried by the student. As each activity is completed, the student removes the picture and places it in the "finished" envelope.

The following is an example of an individual student schedule for the classroom schedule listed above:

Student Arrival

Getting Ready

Morning Circle

Restroom Break

Individual Work Centers

Magnetic Numbers & Blocks

Art and Sensorys

Computers

Recess

The Staff Schedule

Programs for students with autism often involve a variety of staff—teachers, paraprofessionals, and related service personnel. To adequately prepare and organize the roles and responsibilities for each staff member, a daily staff schedule must be created and implemented.

There are a number of reasons for a staff schedule:

1. A written schedule alleviates the need for the teacher to oversee the minute-to-minute responsibilities for each staff member.

2. A carefully designed staff schedule fosters independence among the staff and reduces the need for paraprofessionals to ask for assistance.

3. The schedule identifies specific responsibilities for each staff members from the moment they arrive in the morning until they depart after school.

4. The schedule divides responsibilities among the related service personnel and creates parity among staff members.

5. A staff schedule helps paraprofessionals stretch their skills and acquire more confidence and independence on the job.

The following is a Sample Staff Schedule.

Time/activity	Staff 1	Staff 2	Itinerant
7:30-8:00	Prepare snack-set out items. Prepare Gross motor ctr. Check on new data sheets	Prepare calendar and lunch. Prepare AM circle-materials and reinforcement	
8:00-8:20 Buses, Play & Toilet	Get students off the bus and take to play ctr. Interact w students	Get S. off the bus and take to play ctr. Interact with students	Empty backpacks, check notes from home, put away lunches.
8:20-8:45 Circle Time	Monitor: Sit behind S.-prompt, reinforce and data collection	Monitor: Sit behind S.-prompt, reinforce and data collection	Teach Circle:
8:45-9:30 Centers	Teach-See chart	Teach-See chart	Teach-See Chart
9:30-10:15 Snack and Toilet	Run Snack: set out all items	Run PECS and solicit conversation	Run PECS-monitor library
10:15-10:45 Outside Play	See Chart for daily activity	Break I (15 min)	Occupational Therapist-prepare Obstacle Course
10:45-11:00 Gross Motor	Prepare Centers-check materials and data	Obstacle Course-guide S., reinforce	Run Obstacle Course-

Note the following:

- Members of the classroom staff share responsibilities equally. (A thorough discussion of roles and responsibilities is included at the end of Chapter One.)

- Specific details are provided throughout the day.

- Related service personnel (SLP, OT) are included in the schedule and share staff responsibilities.

- The schedule may remain in effect for one week, but the staff positions should change daily to provide equality and shared decision making for the team.

- All staff are responsible for the maintenance and implementation of the schedule.

- Assign a timekeeper to keep the class and the staff running efficiently and on time.

- If a staff member is anxious about teaching the whole group, allow him or her to teach the last five minutes of a prepared lesson. Slowly increase the time with the entire group while providing supportive feedback.

Helpful Hint: Staff Bulletin Board

Create a staff bulletin board. Include any upcoming special events such as birthdays or holidays. Post reminders about certain students and specific behaviors to reinforce. Use the bulletin board as a reminder for staff to check their schedules. Assign a staff member to update the board. The staff bulletin board may also be used to remind staff of future absences or to leave notes for a substitute teacher.

Conclusion

A well-organized, comprehensive, and consistent schedule is a key element in teaching students with autism. The time invested in preparing a schedule will provide many benefits to both students and staff. The schedule will help new staff members as well as new students with autism assimilate as they arrive throughout the year. Further, new staff members are often unsure of their roles and responsibilities, and a carefully designed, well-written staff schedule allows for independence and a feeling of security.

STAFF ROLES AND RESPONSIBILITIES

New teachers are trained extensively in special education, behavior management, instructional methods, and curriculum development. Yet little training is provided on how to manage or supervise paraprofessionals and other support staff in the classroom. The working relationship between the teacher and the paraprofessional can be one of great support and mutual trust. But unfortunately it can also become destructive and troublesome. All staff should be equally involved in the daily activities and decision making of the classroom in order to increase opportunities for improved staff relationships and to build collaborative multidisciplinary teams. Although there are some legal requirements that can only be fulfilled by a licensed teacher, most of the daily staff roles and responsibilities can be shared among all staff members.

Creating a cooperative working environment requires mutual trust and an egalitarian relationship. Trust takes time and is built through open communication. Unfortunately, many paraprofessionals are hired without input from the licensed teacher, and teachers and paraprofessionals are often thrown together with little opportunity to build a trusting relationship.

Helpful Hint: Staff Meeting

Schedule a weekly staff meeting, even if it is only between the teacher and one paraprofessional. Set aside thirty minutes per week, before or after school, to discuss how the classroom is running and to generate ideas together. A staff meeting is a time to think and plan together. Each person should come to the meeting with some information to share or a concern to discuss. Develop a short agenda so that the meetings are productive and stay on schedule.

Job Description

The lack of clearly defined roles and responsibilities often fosters misunderstanding between and among teachers and paraprofessionals. Teachers often lack the formal training to manage and supervise paraprofessionals, while paraprofessionals often lack educational experience and are uncomfortable in their new positions.

Well written, comprehensive job descriptions empowers the entire staff for a better understanding of the roles and responsibilities. Job descriptions also encourage communication and reduce indecision and conflict. An informal job description allows the teacher and the paraprofessional to discuss their respective strengths and weaknesses and helps identify areas which require future training.

Writing a job description is an important activity for all staff members. Follow these steps:

1. Use a staff team meeting to openly discuss and clarify what each person perceives to be his or her roles and responsibilities within the classroom.

2. Brainstorm and write an informal job description to be used within the classroom.

3. Include a list of all perceived roles and responsibilities. Think outside the box.

Paraprofessionals may be anxious about additional responsibilities, but with appropriate training and support most paraprofessionals can handle the demands of whole group instruction or "Circle Time." The staff schedule and job descriptions provide equal opportunities for staff to share tasks and truly create a collaborative multi-disciplinary team.

Sample Job Description: Paraprofessional

Description: Promotes and supports learning for students with autism. Assists the teacher in creating and promoting a positive learning environment.

Responsibilities:

• Attend weekly staff meetings

• Communicate specific student needs to the teacher

• Assist with toilet schedule

• Prepare classroom materials

• Record and monitor record keeping and data collection

• Support behavioral program

• Provide instruction to large and small groups

- Come to work on time and leave at designated time

- Copy necessary materials

- Inspect and clean toys and activities

- Escort students to and from the bus

- Monitor students on the playground and in the cafeteria

- Share information with the teacher

- Promote appropriate social skills/modeling

- Follow classroom schedule and staff schedule

- Anticipate opportunities for incidental learning

- Use discrete trial instruction

- Attend necessary training and in-service opportunities

Conclusion

Teaching students with autism requires all staff members to share in decision making and responsibilities as a member of a multidisciplinary collaborative team. While the teacher-paraprofessional relationship is both demanding and rewarding, neither may be fully trained to serve as a team member and at the same time, manage the responsibilities of the job.

Not all staff members have to share the same job; we each bring something different to the learning environment. The key element in an effective collaborative relationship is to openly communicate and share responsibilities to create successful results for the students with autism.

 Helpful Hint: Celebrate

Teaching is hard work, so it is important to celebrate the successes of the classroom. Create opportunities to relieve stress as a group and to encourage each other. Bring the staff together and celebrate the dedication of teamwork.

CASE STUDIES:

Read the following case studies and consider the problems as they relate to this chapter.

— Case Study 1 —

Joan is a first year teacher at Braxton Elementary School. She begins the school year in a primary self-contained classroom with eight students with autism. Stephanie and Tina are two paraprofessionals who worked in the classroom during the previous school year and will be working with Joan.

Joan is out-going and anxious to start the school year. She has many new plans to implement and "knows" exactly what she is doing. Joan plans to overhaul the classroom with new décor and a new floor plan. She also implements a highly structured ABA program, which is new to the students and staff. Within the first month of school, Joan is feeling tension between herself and the staff.

Conclusions:

Although Joan is attempting to make some positive changes in the classroom, she must first establish an effective and mutually supportive working environment with the staff. Joan should schedule a staff meeting to discuss the changes to the environment and instruction.

Joan must seek out ideas and input from both paraprofessionals. It is important that Joan establish a shared decision making model with the paraprofessionals. The entire staff should jointly create a plan for environmental changes.

The team should select only one or two modifications in the classroom and slowly introduce new ideas over time as the staff feels comfortable.

— Case Study 2 —

Melissa is in her third year of teaching a self-contained elementary-based program for students with autism. Unfortunately, her assistant from last year had a baby over the summer and will not be returning. The principal hired a new assistant without consulting Melissa and the assistant will begin the school year after the first two weeks of school. John, the new assistant, is in his mid-forties and appears anxious to be working with Melissa, but after a few weeks it is apparent that John keeps his own schedule. Within the first eight weeks of school, John has been absent six days and has been tardy four days by at least thirty minutes. His absences are causing problems in the classroom.

Conclusions:

Melissa must first schedule a meeting with her school administrator to review the policies and procedures for absences within the school district. Melissa should communicate to her school administrator any concerns she may have over John's excessive absences and tardies. The school administrator is ultimately responsible for all staff within the school and must follow appropriate procedures for addressing this problem with John.

Melissa must also schedule a meeting with John to discuss her concerns. Open communication between the teacher and the paraprofessional is the hallmark of an effective working relationship. Melissa must learn to address her concerns without personal judgement. Both Melissa and John should create a mutually agreed upon plan of action for further absences or tardies.

— Case Study 3 —

Jennifer is a one-on-one assistant for Ian, a seven-year-old with Asperger's syndrome. Jennifer also works with Linda, the resource room teacher. Jennifer is extremely diligent about her duties and follows Ian closely. She "jumps in" at the first sign of problems and informs the teachers about all of Ian's problems. Linda only sees Jennifer two periods a day and is not completely aware of the situation in the general education classroom. The word gets around the teacher's lounge that Jennifer is suffocating Ian, and that Linda is not providing appropriate supervision.

Conclusions:

Linda must schedule a meeting with Jennifer to clarify roles and responsibilities. Both Linda and Jennifer should write a list of job responsibilities and review them jointly. This document can be used to assist Jennifer in understanding her responsibilities with Ian.

Linda should also encourage Jennifer to attend any workshops or conferences offered by the school district. It may be helpful for Jennifer to hear new ideas and strategies for working with students with autism. Linda can then follow-up with Jennifer on the information she gained from the training and share new insights as a team.

Lastly, Linda should take some time in the school day to work more closely with Jennifer. Linda can observe Jennifer working directly with Ian and provide praise and objective feedback. Linda must take a more active role in Ian's education because she is ultimately responsible for meeting the goals and objectives of Ian's Individualized Education Plan.

Chapter Two

Designing and Implementing an Appropriate Curriculum

Designing and implementing an appropriate curriculum for students with autism is a continuous process and will evolve throughout the school year as the students' needs change. Both the difficulty and the method for developing an appropriate curriculum for students with autism will vary greatly depending on the severity of the disability. Students with autism may fall anywhere on the spectrum, from mild to severe and each requires an individualized program to meet his unique needs. Some students with autism may be working at grade level and will only require support in social and communication skills. Others may be severely involved and require a program that focuses on functional communication and adaptive skills. There is no cookie cutter curriculum that meets the needs of every student.

The curriculum content for students with disabilities must be broad enough to prepare the student to meet their present and as well as future needs. Modifications to the existing general education curriculum may be necessary by adding supplementary support and services. This requires the classroom teacher or multidisciplinary team to evaluate, plan, and implement the standard curriculum, with modifications, to meet the individual needs of a student with autism. The team must then design a unique program that will address the strengths and weaknesses of the student. The teacher is ultimately responsible for development of a curriculum that not only meets district guidelines and state standards, but more importantly meets the individual needs of the students.

There are several key steps in developing and implementing an appropriate curriculum for students with autism.

Chapter Two will address the following objectives, so the reader should be able to:

- Define curriculum and state the relevance to student outcomes

- Identify and implement the five steps to curriculum development.

- Identify each life domain and its relevance for students with autism.

- State the types of curriculum implementation.

- Define and implement thematic units across each of the life domains.

- Determine the importance of an age appropriate and functional curriculum.

LIFE DOMAINS

We generally refer to certain groups of everyday survival skills as "life domains". These life domains provide a framework for designing and implementing an appropriate curriculum. Here are the working definitions of the life domains:

Cognitive/Academic:

Concept acquisition, skill development in language arts, math, social studies, and science, with a focus on basic facts and rote knowledge, analytical reasoning, and problem solving. Pursuing intellectual tasks.

Speech and Language:

The acquisition of speech and language and the use and understanding of nonverbal gestures for successful communicative interactions.

Play and Leisure:

The use of imitation and symbolic or dramatic play. The use of materials and activities to play independently and participate in interactive activities.

Sensory:

A range of developmental skills of sensory integration including arousal, regulation, modulation, and integration across the natural environments.

Social/Emotional:

The ability to demonstrate social exchanges, to build peer relations and friendships. To recognize and interact through verbal and nonverbal means. Awareness of conversation rules, social interactions, and responses.

Key Concept: Social Skill Development

Including a social skills curriculum for students with ASD is crucial. It is one of the most critical elements in teaching students with autism. It is of little consequence if a student is receiving passing grades in all subject areas but does not have the specific skills to make a friend and communicate with his peers. A comprehensive and purposeful social skills curriculum must be included for all students with autism.

Fine and Gross Motor:

This life domain allows the individual student to maximize specific motor movement for independence. This includes programs for fine motor skills such as pencil grip and gross motor movement such as walking and balance.

Vocational (Secondary):

Competence in the required skills to seek and maintain employment consistent with their needs and abilities. The vocational curriculum also includes the necessary skills to handle work-related social problems.

Although each domain can be defined and evaluated separately, the curriculum and supporting instructional experiences within the classroom will often overlap. For example, during whole group instruction or circle time, the curriculum will include activities and materials for speech and language acquisition, sensory integration, social skills, and academic development. To insure proper attention has been given to each domain, the teacher should review that all domain areas are addressed throughout the school day.

 Helpful Hint: Life Domain Matrix

Review the Life Domain Matrix included in Appendix C. Examine the daily schedule for each student and mark each domain area as it is addressed throughout the day. The purpose of the matrix is to insure that each domain area is adequately addressed during the school day.

CURRICULUM DEVELOPMENT

An appropriate and functional curriculum is defined by all of the instructional experiences and sequential learning objectives of what we teach to students. This not only addresses academic content but also includes social skill development and play and leisure skills. Most states and school districts have adopted standards for curricula along with textbooks that focus on basic skills in language arts, mathematics, and the social sciences. The adopted standards for the general education curriculum are established to meet the needs of typically developing students. However, this academic-oriented focus does not address the needs of students with autism.

An appropriate and functional curriculum for students with disabilities must include such items as social skill development, sensory integration, and play and leisure activities. The general education curriculum provides little opportunity to learn adaptive skills and communication and language skills. If the needs of students with autism are to be adequately addressed, and if we are to increase independence and function of these students in society, then the multidisciplinary team must use a broader and more functional definition of curriculum. This new definition must address the specific needs of students with autism and generalize skills learned to everyday life.

The multidisciplinary team should consider the following outcomes when determining an appropriate curriculum:

1. The curriculum content should have a focus on social skills that are developmentally important to the individual student to function successfully in society.

2. The curriculum should contain all the life domain areas to allow the student to maximize independence at the present and in the future.

3. The curriculum should examine the life-long required skills for the student to b successful in the school and community.

4. The curriculum content should serve a meaningful purpose to the student.

The curriculum is ultimately evaluated based on the essential successful experiences provided to the student in the areas of cognitive, emotional, social, and occupational skills.

For typically developing students, the curriculum is often determined by state standards and district guidelines. Textbook adoption committees and curriculum specialists select an appropriate curriculum and supporting materials. As stated earlier, the general education curriculum does not often meet the educational and emotional needs of students with autism. Therefore, teachers must develop a specially designed curriculum based on available resources and on the needs of the student. Development of a curriculum involves five steps:

1. Curriculum Assessment

2. Developing goals and objectives

3. Determining content and materials

4. Planning and Implementation

5. Curriculum evaluation

1. Assessment of Student Curriculum Needs

The purpose of establishing a systematic curriculum assessment for each student with autism is to identify and create a plan to address the strengths, weakness, and interests across each student's life domains. That can be challenging. Students with autism often have uneven patterns of development within each life domain. Therefore the goal of the assessment process is to determine exactly where those gaps exist and identify the strengths and interests for each student. The multidisciplinary team develops a student profile based on each of the domain areas. Although curriculum assessment may take some time, the outcome will provide the staff with a clear plan of what to teach.

There are a variety of assessment tools available to teachers to assess the student's strengths, interests, and weakness. In deciding which tool to use, the teacher must first consider the age of the student and the availability of the assessment tool. Talk to other special education teachers or the school psychologist about assessment tools appropriate for curriculum planning. The following assessment tools are generally available to classroom teachers and are simple to administer:

Brigance Inventory (Brigance, 1990)

The Brigance is a convenient and easy to use assessment tool which covers a variety of life domains. There are several versions of the Brigance which cover early development, basic skills and employability skills. (Curriculum Associates: 1-800-225-0248)

Vineland Adaptive Behavior Scales (Sparrow et al., 1984)

Also assesses a variety of domains including communication, socialization, daily living skills, and motor skills. The Vineland is often adopted by school districts and should be available through your school psychologist.

Curriculum Based Assessment (CBA)

Tools use objectives in the curriculum as the criteria against which progress is evaluated. A CBA is designed by the teacher based on the current curriculum content for the classroom. A CBA often has broader and more functional use for students with autism because it directly relates to classroom goals and objectives. For example, a teacher who has adopted Navigating the Social World (McAfee, 2002) as a social skills curriculum for the classroom would review the goals that begin each lesson. The teacher would then determine the strengths, interests, and deficits for the child based on the written goals from the curriculum. The teacher has a greater understanding of the results by assessing the curriculum based on specific goals and objectives

Helpful Hint: Shortcuts to Curriculum Assessment

Completing a systematic individualized curriculum assessment for all of the students in your class may seem to be an overwhelming task. However, teachers can save time by considering the following:

- *Conduct a thorough review of the students most recent evaluations to gain as much information as possible about each domain.*

- *Review last year's Individual Education Plan (IEP) and discuss it with last year's teacher.*

- *Select a few domain areas to assess and use with several students in one day.*

- *Use a multidisciplinary approach to assessment.*

- *The teacher is not the only staff member qualified and capable of completing an assessment. Include a variety of staff members in conducting informal assessments. Gather information from parents and include the parents throughout the assessment process.*

After completing the assessment for each student, the teacher and support staff will have a thorough understanding of the student's strengths, interests, and weakness. The team can then develop goals and objectives for each area across the life domains.

2. Developing Goals and Objectives

Most students will enter the program with a completed Individualized Education Plan (IEP), which includes a description of the student's strengths, weaknesses, goals and objectives. Unfortunately, there may be some gaps in the current information which will require further assessment. An IEP usually concentrates heavily on cognitive/academic goals and speech and language, with little emphasis on social/emotional goals or sensory integration skills. Therefore, be sure to check for the following:

- Does the IEP address all life domain areas?

- Will achievement of social/emotional goals in the curriculum adequately provide the student with the necessary social skills?

- Do the social/emotional goals include stress management and coping skills?

- Does the IEP address play and leisure skills?

- Are there goals and objectives for improving sensory integration?

- For students who are nonverbal, are there goals addressing the skills needed for using a functional communication system or augmentative device?

- Do the present goals and objectives address meaningful and long-term skills which are relevant to the future?

If the IEP appears to be comprehensive and includes current assessment information in all life domain areas, the team can begin the process of developing activities and materials for meeting those goals. If the IEP must be adjusted, be sure to follow federal, state and local laws.

A few suggestions to keep in mind when writing annual goals and short term objectives:

- Annual goals are developed for each domain as deemed appropriate by the multidisciplinary team.

- The annual goal should represent a functional learning outcome for the student and should be broadly stated.

- Write three to five short term objectives for each annual goal. Short-term objectives provide the specific skills or steps to meet the goal. They must be observable and measurable, and they must include a standard by which mastery is evaluated.

- Annual goals should be realistically attainable within one-year.

CASE STUDIES

The following case studies provide examples of both curriculum assessment and writing IEP goals and objectives:

— Case Study 1 —

Darin is a third grade student in Mrs. Johnson's general education classroom. Darin is working at grade level and receives consultative services from his resource room teacher, Mrs. Williams. Darin was found eligible for special education services as a student with autism. He attended an integrated preschool and was placed in a regular kindergarten. Although Darin has appropriate language skills, he has few friends and is isolated from his peers. Upon review of his current IEP, Mrs. Williams discovers that Darin has goals and objectives for:

1. Completing assignments,

2. Staying on task and in his seat, and

3. Following teacher directions.

It appears Darin has some deficits in impulse control and in turning in completed assignments. It is apparent to Mrs. Williams that Darin's IEP is lacking in several key areas. For example, Darin's IEP does not contain specific goals and objectives for acquiring appropriate social skills and making friends. The IEP is also lacking in appropriate goals and objectives for play and leisure skills. Mrs. Williams soon realizes that she must conduct an informal curriculum-based assessment and add goals and objectives to Darin's IEP.

Conclusion:

Reconvene the multidisciplinary team and review goals and objectives for social skill development. The team should include goals for initiating conversations with peers and recognizing nonverbal cues.

The multidisciplinary team, including the parents, should also consider creating a circle of friends as a support system for Darin. The circle of friends program can be implemented with a school counselor and a few supportive peers.

Lastly, the team must develop goals and objectives to assist Darin in play and leisure skills. It is important for the team to identify age appropriate play and leisure skills for Darin. Individual sports, such as swimming and karate, can build self-confidence and provide Darin with a life long leisure skill.

Key Concept: Social Skills Development

Although a social skills curriculum may be more challenging to teach than are typical academic areas, it is important that teachers develop goals and objectives. School personnel cannot ignore the social and emotional needs of students with autism because of a lack of personnel available to teach the social skills curriculum and/or a lack of materials.

In the preceding case study, Darin is working at grade level and appears to be mastering his academic skills. But he is not fully benefiting from his education because he lacks social and peer interaction skills. Social skills goals and objectives are needed to help ensure that the student is fully involved in the general education curriculum and is progressing well. The goals also ensure that the student is being prepared for future employment and successful community integration.

— Case Study 2 —

Andrea is a six-year-old student with autism. She has significant delays in communication and in social skills. According to Andrea's most recent psychological evaluation, she functions in the mentally retarded range. Andrea is nonverbal and uses a few pictures to communicate her wants and needs. Andrea has regular temper tantrums and is mildly aggressive towards staff and students when demands are placed on her.

Mr. Collins is Andrea's special education teacher. He is new in his position and is reviewing Andrea's IEP. Although the IEP is current and provides a thorough understanding of Andrea's strengths and deficits, there are no goals and objectives regarding stress management. Mr. Collins is certain that Andrea becomes overstimulated and stressed during the school day. He would like to teach Andrea some calming techniques and include sensory integration techniques within the classroom.

Conclusion:

Mr. Collins should conduct a functional assessment to determine the triggers for Andrea's stress related episodes. The assessment should focus on the specific events that cause Andrea to tantrum and the duration of her outbursts.

Mr. Collins must reconvene the IEP team to add a goal addressing the need for Andrea to utilize a "Break Card" for stress management. The break card should be presented to Andrea during periods of stress.

Mr. Collins should create a "Break Area" in the classroom for students to relax and implement stress management techniques.

Key Concept: Teaching Stress Management

Stressful situations are often a part of the school day for most students. Day to day school schedules and environments can exasperate a student with autism. Nonverbal students, like Andrea, require opportunities to learn coping techniques and stress management skills. School personnel should not assume that a lack of verbal communication diminishes the need for stress management and coping skills. Check to see if the student is able to handle stressful situations and assess to determine the need to teach new skills.

3. Curriculum Content and Implementation

After completion of the assessment and development of written goals and objectives across the life domains, it is time to determine the activities and materials required to achieve written goals and objectives. The teacher and support staff must design the materials and organize the activities in the classroom. The teacher is responsible for coordinating the learning experiences and activities that are suitable for students with varying ability levels.

Thematic Units

A thematic unit integrates the curriculum with materials and activities to a common theme. For example, a teacher may select a recipe to make in the classroom. A variety of subject areas are covered within this theme including reading, math, and leisure skills. Thematic units allow school personnel to program for students with a variety of functioning levels and abilities. Thematic units can assist the teacher in creating a specific unit that can meet the varying needs of the students in the classroom by integrating the curriculum across the various subject areas.

Programs for students with autism will address a variety of functioning levels and abilities. School personnel will often be required to develop and implement a curriculum that encompasses a wide spectrum of ability levels. Thematic units can assist the teacher in creating a specific unit that can meet the varying needs of the students in the classroom.

Principles of Thematic Units:

- A thematic unit relates the materials and activities to a common theme.

- Each theme is integrated across life domains and throughout the schedule.

- Thematic units help students with autism apply their learning experiences to everyday life.

- Thematic units assist the student to build on knowledge being taught in other domain areas.

- Each unit provides structure to the content and allows the concepts to be taught in many ways and across all life domains.

- Thematic units enable the teacher to develop activities and materials, which are purposeful and can be used repeatedly.

Key Concept: Thematic Units

Thematic units provide meaning to disconnected curriculum content for the learner. This method has been widely and successfully used at both the early childhood and elementary school levels. It is important to note that thematic units are also appropriate and effective throughout secondary levels.

Helpful Hints: The World is a Classroom

Not all life domain areas and curricula can be explained inside the classroom, so field trips should be developed as a stimulating and fun activity for a thematic unit. For example, if students have been studying the ocean then give them an opportunity to visit the ocean or water. The staff will often see different aspects of their students when away from the school and exploring the community.

Thematic Units for Elementary and Secondary

Space, Plants, Insects, The Community, Sports, Holidays, Oceans, Olympics, Seasonal Activities, Safety/Traffic, Foods/Nutrition, Health, Transportation, Current Movies/Books

Thematic Unit Planning Form

Step 1. Brainstorm ten to twelve thematic units

Step 2. List each domain area

Step 3. Identify several activities for each domain

Step 4. List all available age-appropriate materials

- Begin by planning three or four thematic units for the school year. Select units with a variety of activities and materials readily available.

- Request donations from families or local businesses.

- Provide center/station plans to all staff.

- Work with other teachers and share materials.

Caution must be taken when considering the topic or theme. Select age-appropriate thematic units that are meaningful to the students and relevant to their lives. For example, if the goal is to learn three new colors and the student is interested in cars, then he can learn his colors through items which involve cars and transportation.

Age Appropriate Materials and Activities

Evaluation of the age-appropriateness of materials and activities is the most important element of curriculum content. To determine if an item or activity is age appropriate, simply observe typically developing students at that same age. If you confirm that this item is being used by other students of the same age, then you can use it in your classroom. Toys and games usually have age recommendations from the manufacturer.

It is not uncommon for a student to become obsessed with a toy or item that is not age appropriate. As professionals, however, we must move the student towards appropriate items of interest. For example, a fourteen-year-old student may enjoy coloring, and coloring may be an appropriate goal for leisure skills and fine motor skills. But the student should not be coloring from a book intended for preschoolers. The staff must provide a coloring book or black and white pages of age appropriate items, e.g., popular musicians, current movies, and/or animals. It is irrelevant that the student may have the developmental ability level of a five-year-old; the student is chronologically fourteen. Refer to Chapter Four for further discussion of how to eliminate rigid obsessions with items that are not age appropriate.

4. Curriculum Implementation

There are several ways to organize and implement the curriculum within the classroom.

Work Stations or Center Based Instruction

First, activities and materials can be organized into workstations or centers. The teacher divides the classroom into stations or centers based on life domains and teaches those specific skills in that station or center. Students rotate through each area and have experiences across the life domains throughout the school day. Each student works on different goals and objectives, although there may be some overlapping.

 Helpful Hints: Workstation Plan

After identifying the specific workstation station and/or centers in the classroom, provide each staff member with a list of suggested activities for that station. A list of the activities, as well as the goals and objectives for that station, is also posted at the station. For example, if the classroom has a clearly defined play and leisure center, the teacher would list all of the goals and objectives to be taught within that center. The final document would then be laminated and posted at that station for all staff to refer to when working with students.

STATION/CENTER PLAN

(Name of Center)

For the Week of: _____

Theme: _____

Goals:

_____

_____

_____

Objectives:

_____

_____

_____

Activities/Materials:

_____

_____

_____

Vocabulary/Communication Temptations:

_____

_____

_____

Individualized Stations or Work Zones

Another option for implementing the curriculum is to create an individualized program where students are assigned specific desks or stations at which they work independently. All materials and activities are specially designed for a particular student and those materials remain in that workstation. This model of implementation limits the student's exposure to a variety of activities but may be necessary for those students who have difficulty transitioning to centers.

Inclusive Classrooms

There are many educational and social goals and objectives that can be adequately addressed in an inclusive classroom with additional school personnel and resources. Teaching across life domains is still a viable option in the general education classroom. The general education teacher, however, must provide instruction in a variety of domain areas that may not be typically addressed in the general education curriculum. There are several easy steps for implementation of the inclusive supported curriculum:

- Create a social skills bulletin board called "How to Be A Friend". Pick one skill a week and discuss practical and concrete strategies with the entire classroom.

- Ask the school counselor to teach a weekly social skills or stress management class. A fifteen to twenty minute lesson per week can provide some necessary skills for stress reduction.

- Identify appropriate social skills as they are observed in the classroom. "Catch a student" implementing an appropriate social skill and concretely describe the target behavior.

- Select a time each day for practicing a relaxation technique, possibly after lunch or recess. Take a minute or two and discuss deep breathing or closing your eyes and counting to ten.

All of these activities will not only benefit the student with autism but will enrich social skills curriculum for other students in the classroom.

5. Curriculum Evaluation

You have now completed the assessment, written goals and objectives and implemented the curriculum. It is now time to evaluate the effectiveness of the curriculum. A critical part of evaluating the effectiveness of the curriculum is through analyzing the data on the rate and quality of student learning. Although data collection techniques and formats will be discussed in Chapter Three, there are other factors which relate specifically to curriculum evaluation which should be considered here.

One aspect in curriculum evaluation is to examine the outcomes through the student's perspective. The staff should consider the following questions when doing this:

- Does the curriculum content and activities make sense to the student?

- Why is this activity or objective important to this particular student?

- What is the purpose of the activity?

- Is the curriculum relevant to their current or future needs?

- Are the activities interesting or fun?

- Is the activity logical and reasonable?

- Does the curriculum content provide meaningful and practical learning opportunities?

By surveying the curriculum content through the perspective of the student, teachers can begin to understand the importance of developing an appropriate and functional curriculum to meet the individual needs of the student.

The staff can also evaluate the effectiveness of the curriculum based on student engagement. Meaningful activities will maintain student interest and help students learn. If the teacher has designed a thematic unit which is expected to last four to six weeks but notices that after three weeks students are losing interest, it is time to select a new theme or change activities.

Curriculum content and activities that lack purpose and meaning lead to boredom, which in turn increases the likelihood of problem behaviors. Putting the same puzzle together day after day will only lead to satiation and boredom. Keep activities novel and current will minimize off-task behaviors. If the staff observes long periods of noncompliant behaviors and a high incidence of problem behaviors, there is a need for further curriculum development.

Chapter Three

Identifying and Implementing Effective Instructional Strategies for Students with Autism Spectrum Disorders

Educating students with autism is an emotionally charged topic because of the mystery surrounding the causes of the disability, and because some of the many teaching options available to parents and teachers are controversial. Thus the identification and implementation of effective instructional strategies for students with autism spectrum disorders (ASD) has also become controversial.

Chapter Three will address the following objectives, so the reader should be able to:

- Understand the various instructional methods available for students with ASD.

- Review current research on effective methods.

- Identify the principles of Applied Behavior Analysis (ABA).

- Implement the components for discrete trial instruction.

- Conduct an ABA program in a variety of settings.

- Review the principles and guidelines for incidental teaching methods.

- Understand the steps for generalization of new skills.

- Review appropriate inclusive strategies.

As with all areas of effective programming, instructional strategies and methods should be designed and implemented based on the needs of the student. The methods and techniques provided in this chapter are not intended to exclude other methods which may be appropriate for students with autism. The multidisciplinary team should determine the most effective methods based on the needs of the individual student.

Instructional Strategies

Students with ASD require instructional strategies that have been specifically designed to meet their needs. School personnel should consider the unique needs of the individual student when determining an appropriate instructional method.

Over the past decade, a variety of instructional methods and strategies for students with autism have been promoted as effective. Although the following list is not exhaustive, it gives some idea of what has been developed and reported to be valid for students with autism.

- Touch therapy
- Holding therapy

- Music therapy
- Sensory integration

- Social Stories™
- Applied behavior analysis

- TEACCH
- Floor time

- Facilitated communication
- Incidental teaching

- Auditory integration
- Visual strategies

- Video modeling

School teams have the formidable task of determining appropriate methods for teaching each of the life domains and meeting the individual needs of students with autism. Since no single instructional method has proven successful for all students in teaching all of the life domain areas, school personnel may have difficulty in developing an appropriate program for students with autism. Multidisciplinary teams should consider the following guidelines when selecting appropriate instructional methods:

1. Review all research that supports the implementation of the selected method.

2. Determine the nature of the research (quantitative vs. qualitative) and the population for which it was intended.

3. Review specific outcomes for effectiveness on students at various ability levels.

4. Review longitudinal studies conducted in school settings.

5. Network with other teachers and get a first hand account of effective instructional strategies.

6. Collect data to determine the effectiveness of the chosen instructional method. Check if the methods are developmentally appropriate.

After reviewing the current research on instructional methods, some school personnel may choose to implement an "eclectic approach" to teaching students with autism. This method borrows parts from several teaching methods to create a unique and individualized instructional strategy. An eclectic approach requires a clear understanding of available methods and a thorough knowledge of their implementation. Caution must be given for selecting an eclectic approach in order to prevent a "hodge-podge" of instructional methods with no clear understanding of the specific techniques and components. It is important that the multidisciplinary team select an instructional approach that has been scientifically proven effective for students with autism.

To assist school personnel in their selection of effective instructional methods for students with autism, two specialized methods for teaching students with autism will be reviewed. Chapter Three will review a "school friendly" variation of Applied Behavior Analysis and Incidental Teaching methods. By concentrating on these two methods, teachers will have available a continuum of instructional options ranging from a highly structured direct teaching method to one that is more student directed and experiential. There are many opportunities throughout the school day to employ each method based on the individual needs of the student and the life domain being targeted.

Key Concept: Accountability

It is appropriate to use a varied approach to teaching the curriculum for individual students. Teachers must be able to identify specific methods being implemented and exactly how those methods are documented. School personnel are accountable for the methods they choose as well as the outcome for the individual student.

Applied Behavior Analysis

Applied Behavior Analysis (ABA) is one of many instructional methods used for teaching various skills and adaptive behaviors. This method has been available to school personnel for decades and is based on the early research of B. F. Skinner. Skinner researched extensively on the operant relationship between a stimulus and response. The principles of Applied Behavior Analysis are based on operant conditioning or positive reinforcement and consequences.

Applied Behavior Analysis has been carefully researched over the last twenty years and found to be a scientifically valid and reliable intervention for improving the learning rates and outcomes for students with autism. There have been a variety of supporters for the use of an intensive behavioral approach, including The Surgeon General Report, the National Academy of Sciences, and the New York State Department of Health. Refer to the Appendix for a list of resources.

The principles of ABA are based on operant conditioning or positive reinforcement and consequences. Simply stated:

> *ABA is an instructional method applied in real world settings, such as classrooms, and breaks down a skill or behavior into small parts that are observable and measurable with the inclusion of data collection and analysis.*

DTI (Discrete Trial Instruction)

Applied Behavioral Analysis uses a variety of strategies such as token economies, behavioral contracts, and the most common form of ABA for students with autism, Discrete Trial Instruction (DTI), also referred to as Discrete Trial Therapy and/or Discrete Trial Training.

Discrete Trial Instruction (DTI) is a specific ABA approach based on behavioral theory which suggests behaviors or skills are learned responses to reinforcement or consequences.

Principles of DTI include:

- Teacher-student interaction is high

- Active student engagement

- Sequenced and structured materials and activities

- Tasks or skills are broken into small measurable steps by completing a task analysis

- Utilizes powerful motivation or reinforcement

- Provides corrective and informational feedback

- Gives the student many chances to learn a new skill, increased repetition

- Strong emphasis on data collection

- Provides clear and concrete instructions

- Maximizes student participation and learning outcomes

Discrete Trial Instruction enables the teacher to teach any area of the curriculum more effectively.

 Key Concept: The Evolutionary Process of ABA and DTI

Because ABA and DTI have been used for students with developmental disabilities for many years, they have been refined and improved. Many professionals once believed that ABA was too robotic and inflexible to be an effective tool for

classrooms, while Discrete Trial Instruction has evolved to be more teacher and student friendly. The current DTI is more natural, student centered, and fun.

Before Starting consider the following guidelines for DTI:

1. Take the necessary time and build a positive rapport with each student. Students are more motivated to work with adults who take time to know them and understand their likes and dislikes.

2. Always strive for success. If the student fails at one attempt, analyze the instruction, reinforcement, and/or curriculum, then try again.

3. The identified objectives and activities must be meaningful to the student to maximize learning.

4. Increase generalization by teaching skills across a variety of settings, materials, and staff.

Steps to Discrete Trial Instruction

Discrete Trial Instruction is made up of five basic components, which can be easily implemented by all school personnel.

1. Instruction

2. Prompt—when necessary

3. Response or behavior from the student

4. Reinforcement or feedback

5. Between-trial Interval

When all staff have been appropriately trained in each of the following components, DTI is an effective instructional method for teaching students with autism.

Step 1. The Instruction

The instruction or stimulus is a clearly defined beginning for each trial or learning opportunity. In the ABA field this is often referred to as the discriminative stimulus or SD. (Refer to *A Work in Progress, Leaf & McEachin, 1999* for a further discussion of discriminative stimulus). When utilizing an ABA approach, school personnel are trained to provide clear instructions to the student.

Rules for Selecting an Instruction:

• The instruction may be a verbal or visual cue, or a gesture.

• Give the instruction one time.

• Either positive reinforcement or feedback follows every instruction.

• Caution: Do not always use the same instructions for a desired task. Vary the instruction in order to decrease rigidity and to keep it natural.

• The complexity of the instruction is based on the student's ability to comprehend and respond appropriately. For example, when identifying colors the instruction for a student with limited skills may be: "What color?" or for a more advanced student, "Tell me the color of the car."

- The instruction should clearly articulate the desired skill. The instruction should lack vagueness or irrelevant information.

- Instructions should be stated firmly without hesitation. Be careful not to state an instruction in the form of a friendly request. For example: "Would you hang your coat in the locker, please?" The student may say "No" or refuse this request. Rather, the instruction should be stated as a fair but firm demand, "Hang your coat in the locker."

 Helpful Hint: Create an "Instructional Cheat Sheet"

Develop an instructional cheat sheet for each domain area to enable all staff members in implementing DTI in the classroom. Simply identify the objectives being taught for each domain area and give examples of instructions for the staff to use. Leave blank spaces to add new instructions.

Sample Instructions:

Objective:

When given three different colored objects, the student will receptively identify the color green with 90% accuracy.

Instructions:

Touch green, Show me green, Where's green?, Give me green, Point to green, Pick-up green

Step 2. Prompt—But Only When Necessary

A prompt is any additional assistance given to the student to elicit a correct response to the instruction. The goal for each trial is a correct student response; therefore a prompt may be necessary when teaching a new skill. Prompts are always planned and should be used cautiously. Prompts are added to the instruction to increase the likelihood of a correct response from the student.

Rules For Prompting:

- Prompts are only effective if they produce the correct response from the student.

- Prompts are always given with the instruction, not with the feedback or reinforcement.

- Repeating the instruction and prompt several times only teaches the student to wait and not respond the first time.

- A specific plan should be developed to fade prompts gradually.

- If the prompt is unsuccessful at eliciting the correct response, consider giving a more intrusive prompt.

Key Concept: Do Not Create Prompt Dependence

Prompt dependence occurs when a student has received multiple prompts over a long period of time and consequently only responds to the prompt and not the initial instruction. All staff must be careful to use prompts only when necessary and to have a plan for fading or reducing prompts immediately or to use less intrusive prompts.

There are many different kinds of prompts and they should be considered on a hierarchy from least to most intrusive. The staff member must determine the most appropriate prompt for each student for meeting the objective.

Helpful Hint: Create Staff Videos

To insure that staff members are not providing inadvertent prompts, each person should videotape themselves implementing DTI in the classroom. Select one day a week for videotaping short instructional sessions. Review the videotapes at your weekly staff meetings. Have each staff member critique the accuracy of the instruction and the use of prompts. Be sure all staff members feel comfortable being videotaped and create an opportunity for a shared learning experience.

Step 3. Student Response or Behavior

Following the instruction and a possible prompt, the student is given adequate time to respond. There is some discussion in the ABA field as to the appropriate amount of time to allow the student to respond, but the general rule of thumb is three to five seconds. A correct response may take longer for some students who have processing difficulties and who are learning a new skill. Also, if the student is clearly unable to respond or if maladaptive behavior is interfering with the student response, the staff should quickly provide informational feedback and move on to the next trial.

Rules for Student Response:

- Allow sufficient time for the student to respond.

- Vary response time according to the individual needs of the student.

- Be sure the response meets the criteria for that particular objective and that it is clearly understood by all staff.

- Quickly end the trial if a problem behavior interferes with a correct response.

Step 4. Consequence

Consequence does not mean punishment. The consequence is simply what happens after the student responds. In fact, there should be no negative reaction or punishment for an incorrect response. The consequence will vary depending on whether the student responded correctly, responded incorrectly, or responded correctly with a prompt. A consequence may take the form of reinforcement or informational feedback, depending on the student's response.

Consequence: Reinforcement

Positive and negative reinforcement is the cornerstone of an effective ABA program. Although most neurotypical students are self-motivated to learn, students with autism often require external motivation to increase their rate of learning. Therefore, school personnel must identify a list of reinforcers that can be easily incorporate into every teaching opportunity.

Using external motivation should not be considered bribery. Reinforcement is always contingent upon the student providing a correct response or exhibiting an appropriate behavior. Reinforcement should never be used to entice a student into working or to reduce a behavior problem once it has already occurred. Reinforcement, both positive and negative, is only implemented after the student has successfully completed the task and met the specified objective.

Key Concept: Reinforcement For All

The goal of DTI is to increase the likelihood of a correct response, thereby meeting the criteria of that learning objective. The most important element for insuring a correct response is the development of reinforcement for each individual student.

Both positive and negative reinforcement are used to increase or maintain adaptive behaviors and decrease maladaptive behaviors. In order to determine the effectiveness of a particular reinforcer, the staff should consider whether that reinforcer helps to maintain or increase the targeted behavior. There are many guidelines for effective implementation of reinforcement. Specific reinforcement principles will be discussed further in Chapter Four.

Helpful Hint: Creating Reinforcement Baskets

All students require some type of reinforcement. Create a reinforcement basket or bin that is customized to the specific likes and dislikes of each student in the classroom. A reinforcement basket can simply be a small bucket, plastic bin, or a

canvas bag that portable and follows the student across settings. The staff should
identify a variety of tangible reinforcers and activities for each student. The
reinforcement basket is used by the staff and available to the student throughout
the day after successful learning occurs.

Consequence: Informational and Corrective Feedback

If the student responds incorrectly to the instruction, reinforcement is withheld and
feedback is given to the student. Informational feedback is a simple statement provided to
the student to let him know that he was incorrect.

Rules for Informational Feedback:

• Provide feedback in a neutral voice.

• Provide information to the student as to the required behavior.

• Feedback should not be punitive.

• Feedback should also include the identification of appropriate behaviors
exhibited by the student.

• Whether the student responds correctly or incorrectly, the staff should be
consistent with the consequence.

Suggestions for Informational Feedback:

"No"; "That was close, try again"; "Not quite, look at me"; "No, keep your
hands on your lap", "Pretty close, sit quietly." "Almost, great sitting."

Step 5: Between-Trial Interval

The pause between trials is an important component in DTI. The between-trial interval teaches the student to wait and allows the staff to collect data and gather materials. It also provides time for the student to use a tangible reinforcer.

Too often the teacher will speed up the pace of the discrete trial process in order to maintain student attention and momentum. This is not effective. Moving too quickly between trials can easily overwhelm a student who may need some processing time. Effective DTI should be paced for optimal learning by the student.

Putting it all Together

At first glance Discrete Trial Instruction may appear to be difficult to implement in the classroom. With practice and teamwork, however, the process becomes more natural. The entire staff can implement each DTI component throughout the school day. Whether in the classroom or on the playground, the five steps to DTI can be easily maintained. The more often the staff uses the DTI components, the more consistently and frequently the student will learn.

DTI is an effective method for teaching many skills across the life domains. It allows the teacher to teach a variety of skills more effectively.

Domain: Self-Help Skills, Setting a Table

Instruction: "Pick up four Forks"

Prompt: Gesture: point to forks

Response: Student picks up forks.

Consequence: Verbal Reinforcement: "Excellent, you picked up the forks"

Between-trial Interval: Data Collection

This example depicts a scenario for utilizing discrete trial instruction for teaching functional skills.

Frequently asked Questions about DTI

1.   **How often do you provide reinforcement?**

At first, reinforcement should be provided after each successful trial. Gradually, reinforcement should be delayed and be faded (given less and less). The goal is to make the student self-motivating.

2.   **How many trials should you implement in each session?**

As a general rule, there are ten trials for each objective. But given time restraints and classroom demands, that number can be flexible. Just remember that it may take ten to twenty correct responses for a student to internalize and generalize one small step in a new skill.

3.   **When do you collect data?**

Data collection can take place during the between-trial interval, or at the end of a session. The team may decide to take estimated data during a break in the schedule.

4.   What do you do when the student is noncompliant?

Many of the problem behaviors associated with noncompliance are addressed in Chapter Four. There may be many reasons that a student is noncompliant. The team must determine what purpose the behavior serves for the student. Noncompliance may require an adjustment in the activity or it may require a more powerful reinforcer. Do not allow noncompliant students to have access to their reinforcement. First, end the trial with informational feedback. Second, provide an instruction with which the student is very likely to comply. For example, clapping hands. Finally, provide reinforcement for compliance and build behavioral momentum.

5.   What do you do when the student does not want to give up the reinforcer?

Teachers often state that it is hard to give a student an item for reinforcement and then expect to get the tangible item back. For example, John is highly motivated by Legos. After correctly matching concepts, John is reinforced with Legos to play with for a couple of minutes. The teacher finds that John does not want to give the Legos back when it is time to work. In this example, the teacher and staff must teach John that even though he must give up the Legos, he can easily earn them back after working on the stated objectives. John will eventually understand the cause and effect of receiving reinforcement and will be more willing to cooperate. At first, the staff may need to reinforce John after every trial, then gradually increase the number of trials before John receives the Legos.

DTI in Group Settings

Discrete trial instruction is an effective instructional strategy that can be implemented during one-to-one instruction and small group instruction. Positive results can be gained in small groups while maintaining active student engagement and increased teacher response. According to Leaf and McEachin (1999), DTI can be implemented during small group instruction using any of the following approaches:

Sequential:

- Small group instruction

- The entire 5 steps to DTI are given to each student individually while the other students wait for their turn.

- The instruction may change in complexity to adjust for the ability level of the student.

- Teacher selects students randomly.

- Provide both individual reinforcement and whole group reinforcement.

Sequential Case Study

Six students are sitting in a semi-circle. The teacher is in front of the group and one paraprofessional sits behind the group for support. Utilizing sequential DTI, the teacher instructs Student #1 to "Stand up and say good morning" After student #1 responds appropriately, the teacher provides the student with a tangible reinforcement and verbal praise. The teacher moves to Student #4, "What color is your shirt?" Student #4 responds and is provided feedback. Next, the teacher asks Student #2, "What did you have for breakfast?" Again, the student responds and the teacher provide reinforcement. The teacher moves throughout the group utilizing a sequential approach to Discrete Trial Instruction.

Choral:

- All students are given one instruction.

- The instruction should be appropriate for all students to follow.

- Students respond as a group.

- Provide both individual and group reinforcement.

Choral Responding Case Study

The teacher has created laminated photographs of each student and staff member. Utilizing a choral responding approach, the teacher holds up the photograph to the entire group and asks, "Who is it?" The students are expected to verbally identify the person in the picture. The teacher and paraprofessional respond with both informational feedback and reinforcement to the group. If one or two students do not respond correctly, the teacher can provide additional assistance to the student.

Overlapping:

- An overlapping approach requires the staff to be extremely adept in the methods for DTI.

- Student #1 is given an instruction that requires a longer period to complete or respond.

- While Student #1 is working on the task, the teacher provides an instruction to Student #2 in the group.

- As Student #1 completes the task, the teacher provides the correct consequence and ends the trial with either reinforcement or feedback.

- This approach is very effective when working with students with various ability levels.

Overlapping Case Study

With a group of six students, the teacher provides Student #1 with an instruction:

"Write the date and today's lunch menu on the board." As Student #1 is working on this task, the teacher utilizes a choral approach with the rest of the group.

The teacher states, "Repeat the days of the week." Upon completion of the days of the week, the teacher provides whole group reinforcement by blowing bubbles with the five remaining students. Student #1 correctly completes his task and returns to his seat and the teacher reinforces with social praise and a high-five.

Small group instruction is a viable option for utilizing discrete trial instruction. With a little practice and feedback, all staff members can efficiently implement DTI with small groups and one-to-one instruction.

Conclusion

Applied Behavior Analysis and Discrete Trial Instruction are important instructional methods for teaching students with autism. DTI is focused on breaking skills into small parts and sequentially teaching the necessary skills to the student. DTI emphasizes a direct instruction approach with a high degree of student engagement and positive learning outcomes.

Incidental Teaching Methods

The goal for learning any new skill is to generalize the skill across settings, people, materials, and time. That is, to be able to use the skill in everyday life. In order to accomplish this goal, a continuum of intervention strategies must be implemented. It is important for the student to progress from a highly structured and restricted intervention to more natural and independent learning environments. Following the guidelines for DTI will enable the student to learn the basic skills with a focus on generalizing newly mastered skills. While Incidental Teaching Methods encourage self-inquiry and a more natural learning approach.

Principles of Incidental Teaching Methods:

1.   Student initiated and student centered.

2.   Supports the generalization of newly acquired skills in natural environments.

3.   Permits a more interactive learning environment.

4. Allows the student to initiate his own learning

5. Encourages exploration and experiential learning.

6. Provides a more multidimensional learning experience for the student.

7. Curriculum content and activities are based on the specific wants and needs of the student.

8. Nonverbal students can initiate through gestures and visual cues.

10 Steps to Incidental Teaching

Step 1.   Arrange the environment for the student, to include tempting toys and activities.

Step 2.   Place toys and favorite activities just beyond the student's reach, but still within eyesight to encourage the student to request. Or, withhold pieces to a favorite toy or activity i.e. sabotage a toy to force a request.

Step 3.   Provide the student with an object that is out of context for the activity. For example, hand him a toothbrush during snack time.

Step 4.   Allow the student to make choices between several activities

Step 5.   Use favorite reinforcement activities or tangibles to initiate a response.

Step 6.   Begin a favorite song or activity and then pause and wait for the student to respond.

Step 7.   Engage in student directed play and interact with each student based on student initiation.

Step 8.   All staff members must be ready to respond and reinforce student initiated behaviors.

Step 9.   Staff responses should include opportunities for students to use expanded language or request assistance.

Step 10.   Data collection occurs when the student initiates a behavior or generalizes a newly mastered skill.

Incidental teaching methods are particularly useful when teaching social skills, self-help skills, and communication and language. This approach takes skills learned through direct instruction and generalizes them to more complex and natural environments.

 Helpful Hint: Staff Challenge "Catch Students Using Targeted Skills"

Create a challenge for the staff to provide incidental teaching opportunities. Take a poll to see who can catch the most student initiations in one day and award a prize.

Conclusion

Identifying and implementing appropriate instructional strategies are central components to teaching students with autism. After building the foundation on a positive learning environment and an appropriate curriculum, school personnel must then focus on day-to-day classroom teaching.

Discrete Trial Instruction and Incidental Teaching Methods provide the multidisciplinary team with the necessary tools for teaching across the life domain areas and at various ability levels. Implementing both strategies will provide the appropriate instruction necessary for learning and generalizing of new skills.

Chapter Four

Developing Effective Behavior Programming and Reinforcement Strategies

Effective teaching strategies for students with autism requires developing a systematic program for addressing problem behaviors. Students with autism will often exhibit a wide variety of challenging behaviors including physical aggression, self-injury, tantrums, and noncompliance. These behaviors are disconcerting to the staff and should be resolved. The following chapter on developing effective behavior intervention programs is often the most important step for the classroom teacher and the success of the student.

Chapter Four will address the following objectives, so the reader should be able to:

- Review the elements of a functional assessment.

- Develop and write a behavior intervention plan.

- Identify the principles of active programming.

- Teach replacement skills.

- Review environmental controls.

- Implement compliance training.

- Plan reactive programming.

- Develop a crisis management plan.

An effective program for managing problem behaviors focuses on two main strategies:

1. Principles of Proactive Programming:

Highly effective programs for students with autism emphasize proactive strategies for reducing problem behaviors and teaching replacement skills.

- Proactive programs assume the problem behavior serves a purpose for the student and attempts to teach alternative and replacement skills which serve the same function.

- Proactive programs modify the antecedents and environmental controls.

- Proactive programs begin by determining the function of the maladaptive behavior for the student.

- Proactive programs seek replacement behaviors for the maladaptive behavior.

2. Principles of Reactive Programs:

Systematic reactive programs can effectively decrease the frequency and duration of problem behaviors. Unfortunately, most classrooms for students with autism focus entirely on reactive programming.

- Reactive programs wait for the maladaptive behavior to occur and then respond with a punishment.

- Reactive programs focus on the consequences of the behavior.

- Reactive programs may ultimately reinforce the maladaptive behavior.

- Reactive programs do not significantly or permanently change maladaptive behaviors.

A comprehensive intervention program for students with autism will provide a careful balance between both a proactive and reactive program. This involves conducting a thorough functional assessment and the development of an appropriate behavior intervention plan.

Proactive Program

Functional assessment is the first step in a proactive program. It begins the process of understanding the purpose of the student's behavior and what the student is trying to communicate. The goal of a functional assessment is to identify the purpose and the effect of a target behavior by examining the function for the student.

An effective functional assessment is built on several assumptions. The first assumption is that the problem behavior serves a function for the student. Students exhibiting problem behaviors are using a functional approach to communication to achieve a specific outcome. Therefore, school personnel must conduct a functional assessment to thoroughly understand function of the behavior for that student.

The second assumption is that if a student is repeating a problem behavior, then the consequence of the behavior has been reinforced for that student in the past. Each of us tends to repeat behaviors that are positively reinforced.

The last assumption is that students exhibiting problem behaviors often do not know the correct adaptive skills, or they have not been effectively reinforced for displaying appropriate adaptive behaviors.

 Key Concept: Completing a Functional Assessment

According to IDEA, a functional assessment is performed "when a child's behavior impedes his or her learning or that of others." Because autism is based on the identification of behaviors, in nearly all cases a student with autism would

require a functional assessment. If the IEP team decides that the student does not exhibit behavior that impedes his learning, an informal functional assessment should be performed for staff planning. ALL students with autism should have a functional assessment and a written behavioral intervention plan completed.

Functional Assessment Made Easy

Whether mandated through an IEP team or conducted as an informal assessment by the classroom staff, a functional assessment can be conducted efficiently and easily with the right tools:

Step 1. Define Target Behavior

First, define an observable and measurable target behavior. The problem behavior targeted for a functional assessment will vary greatly depending on the student. The team may choose to target a behavior which can be easily corrected before moving to more challenging behaviors. Targeting lesser behaviors may build success for the student and staff and make changing more challenging behaviors easier.

Conversely, if behaviors are harmful to the student or others, the team may choose to work on several behaviors at once. All identified target behaviors must be clearly defined and measurable to ensure consistency across settings.

Key Concept: Redefining Problem Behaviors

School personnel must shift their view from defining problem behaviors as deficits and weaknesses to an assumption that the student's behavior is a response to his environment. When viewed from the student's perspective, the student is communicating through the problem behavior in a functional manner. Therefore, school personnel must create and teach more adaptive behaviors to meet the student's communication needs.

Step. 2 Information Gathering

Collect information from a variety of sources. The team may interview teachers, parents, and related service personnel who work with the student. Interview data focuses on the antecedents and consequences of the behavior. Interview adults who have a significant relationship with the student and who can contribute to defining the target behavior and function.

Information may also be collected through direct observation. Observations focus on the frequency, duration, and intensity of the target behavior. (Refer to Chapter Five for Data Collection Forms) Observations should occur in the natural settings where the target behavior is exhibited. Direct observations also include an analysis of environmental factors that may contribute to the maladaptive behavior.

The team should consider the following when observing the environment:

- Presence of extraneous environmental stimuli

- Noise level

- Interactions with classmates

- Teacher proximity

- Classroom layout and décor

- Predictability and consistency of schedules

- Level of adult assistance

- Access to communication devices

- Classroom activities are age appropriate

- Activities target appropriate skills

- Activities are of interest to the student

- Adequate feedback and reinforcement

Physiological factors are the last area of data collection which may influence problem behaviors. Students with autism often have potential medical issues that are causing an increase in maladaptive behaviors. Physiological areas to be considered in a functional assessment:

- Diet and nutrition

- Sleep patterns and fatigue

- Medication side effects

- Sickness

- Stress outside of the classroom

It is important to carefully consider how these variables influence problem behaviors. If the student is hungry or thirsty and has no functional communication system, the outcome will be irritability and an increase in problem behaviors. The classroom team can effectively address these issues and reduce further problem behaviors.

Step 3. Developing a Hypothesis

The third step in a functional assessment is to review the data and identify the function of the problem behavior. The function of problem behaviors varies with each student. The following are a few common functions and applicable questions to be addressed by the team:

Escape/Avoidance

- Is the task too difficult?

- Is the student bored?

- Does the behavior start when a request or demand is made?

- Does the activity take too long?

- Is the classroom too noisy?

- Does the behavior stop when the student is removed from the activity?

Attention

- Is the student receiving adequate attention for NOT displaying the problem behavior?

- Are other students receiving more attention?

- Is the student alone for long periods?

- Does the student exhibit the behavior when they are alone?

- Does the behavior occur to get a reaction?

Power/Control

- Is the student given choices in the classroom?

- Are there opportunities for the student to take a break?

- Does the behavior stop after the student receives a desired object?

Communication

- Does the student have a functional and reliable communication system?

- Is the student provided with the necessary equipment to communicate wants and needs?

- Does the behavior seem to be a way for the student to ask for help?

Stress/Frustration

- Is the student stressed?

- Does the student have adequate skills to release stress in an appropriate manner?

• Is the classroom environment chaotic?

• Does the student seem calm or relaxed after the problem behavior has stopped?

Self-Stimulation or Sensory Stimulation

• Is the behavior part of the stereotypical pattern of behaviors?

• Is the environment producing adequate stimulation?

• Does the student have frequent opportunities for sensory integration?

• Does the student repeat the behavior when alone?

• Does the student appear unaware of his surroundings?

The multidisciplinary team examines the information collected and develops a written statement regarding the function of the behavior. A clear hypothesis statement is written in a positive manner, based on facts from information gathering. The following are examples of hypothesis statements:

• Morning circle is too long for Jonathan, and he bites other students to escape the task.

• Samantha refuses to complete her morning math work because she requires additional adult assistance. When the teacher is helping other students, Samantha attempts to run out of the room to get immediate attention from the teacher.

• Carlos screams and cries when his mother is late picking him up and when his communication board is not available.

- When Stephen goes to the cafeteria with the fifth grade class, he pushes other students and runs down the hallway to be first in line and to avoid waiting with the other students.

Each hypothesis statement identifies the target behavior and provides an "informed guess" as to the function of the behavior for the student.

Key Concept: Functional Communication

Students with Autism Spectrum Disorders often have severe deficits in expressive language and communication skills. Therefore, there is an immense need for alternative communication systems. Augmentative and alternative communication devices allow the student to communicate and respond to the environment. Problem behaviors will only persist or increase if the student is unable to communicate basic needs.

Helpful Hint: Student Profile: Functional Communication Assessment

As part of the Student Profile, include a quick communication assessment which asks the following questions. Can the student readily access a communication device to:

- Express his wants and needs

- Request help

- Protest or refuse

- Initiate a social interaction

- Ask for affection or comfort

- Play act or pretend

If the answer is "no" to any of these questions, immediately involve your speech and language pathologist and augmentative communication specialist to create or purchase a device which will meet the student's communication needs.

Step 4: Developing a Behavior Intervention Plan

The behavioral intervention plan is a written document that includes:

- An operational definition of the target behavior.

- Summary of the relevant data.

- Written hypothesis statement stating the function of the behavior.

- List of modifications to the environment.

- Teaching replacement or alternative behaviors.

- Criteria or outcome evaluation.

- Consequence strategies: crisis intervention plan and reactive programming.

Most school districts have developed appropriate forms to be used for a written behavior intervention plan. If no form is readily available, the teacher can easily create an individualized plan for use in the classroom. The following behavior intervention plan may be used as an informal tool and as part of the student profile.

Behavior Intervention Plan

A	B	C
• Antecedent • Context • Environment • Before the behavior occurs	• Observable • Measurable • Specific • Target behavior	• Consequence • After the behavior occurs • Function to the student

Hypothesis Statement: (When this occurs .../The student does ...../In order to ....)

_____

_____

_____

Environmental Modifications:

_____

_____

_____

Reinforcement Hierarchy:

_____

_____

_____

Proactive Plan

Replacement Skills

Describe the specific replacement skill for the student.

Who is Responsible

Identify who is responsible for teaching the replacement skill.

Method of Instruction

Identify how the skill will be taught to the student.

When? Data Collection

Identify a timeline for evaluation and data collection methods.

Reactive Program

In the event the target (maladaptive behavior) occurs, describe the specific consequence strategies (i.e. extinction, response cost, or time-out) including a crisis plan:

1. _____

2. _____

3. _____

4. _____

5. _____

Define the long-term behavioral goal:

_____

_____

The multidisciplinary team must consider the following proactive strategies in the behavior intervention plan:

1. Teaching replacement or alternative behaviors.

2. Environmental modifications.

Teaching Replacement Skills

Teaching replacement skills or alternative behaviors assumes the student's problem behavior is meeting a need for the student and that the student may not have the skills required for more adaptive behaviors. The replacement behavior, therefore, must be as effective and powerful as the maladaptive behavior.

For example, if Zachary receives immediate and intense attention from the teacher for biting another student, the new replacement behavior must also give Zachary the same immediate and intense attention from the teacher. Teaching Zachary to raise his hand and wait several moments for the teacher's attention will not be an effective alternative skill.

Key Concept: Teaching Replacement Skills

Teaching the desired replacement skill should result in:

1. Meeting the same function or purpose for the student

2. Teaching a skill that can be implemented across settings

3. The new replacement skill results in an efficient and effective alternative for the student

Teachers may implement a variety of instructional methods for teaching replacement behaviors to students with autism. While discrete trial instruction and incidental teaching methods are highly effective strategies in teaching replacement behaviors, the classroom staff can also implement other strategies including shaping, differential reinforcement, and token economies.

Shaping

Shaping is a proactive strategy used to teach new behaviors or skills. Shaping builds on current student skills and reinforces the student's effort to approximate the replacement behavior. Students are reinforced for minor improvements to learning a new skill. Shaping procedures enable the classroom staff to gradually teach a new skill and provide positive reinforcement throughout the learning process.

Guidelines for Implementing Shaping Procedures:

- List all necessary steps to take the student from his/her present level to the desired behavior. Complete a task analysis.

- Highly quality reinforcement is provided every time the student exhibits an approximation of the alternative behavior.

- Reinforcement may occur at different rates depending on the student's ability level and learning rate.

- At first it may be necessary to heavily reinforce all approximations to the alternative behavior.

For example, Jared has difficulty standing in line for long periods with the entire class. An alternative behavior for Jared is for him to stand on a pair of colored feet while waiting in line. Because Jared does not currently have this skill, the teacher must break the task down into small steps. The following steps are taught over a period of time to shape Jared's behavior:

1. Colored feet are placed on the floor by the classroom door.

2. Jared is prompted to place his feet on the colored feet and wait 5 seconds. Jared is highly reinforced for his effort of standing on the feet.

3. After Jared has successfully mastered standing on the colored feet for 5 seconds, the teacher increases the length of time required of the student.

4. Jared must now stand on the colored feet for ten seconds to receive high-quality reinforcement.

5. After each approximation has been mastered, the student receives reinforcement.

6. The final step is for Jared to wait in line with the rest of the class.

Shaping procedures provide built-in opportunities for immediate reinforcement as the student is learning a new skill. Although shaping procedures can be time-consuming, it provides a practical approach to teaching replacement behaviors.

Token Economies

The token economy is a useful and practical strategy for reinforcing and teaching new behaviors. Token economy systems can also be an effective proactive procedure for managing problem behaviors. Token economy systems target a new behavior and provide an object or token in exchange for the presence of the desired behavior. The tokens can then be traded for a predetermined reinforcement. Token economies are flexible and easy to use across settings.

Guidelines for Implement a Token Economy:

- Select a tangible token that is durable and easy to manipulate. Stickers, coins, points, and buttons are appropriate tokens.

- The token is used as visual evidence to the student that he or she has achieved a desired behavior.

- Determine the criteria and rules for successful task completion.

- Select high quality reinforcement that will be exchanged for the token. Selection of reinforcement will be discussed later in Chapter Four.

- Establish the ratio of exchange for the tokens and the reinforcement. Initially, the reinforcement should be provided immediately after the first token has been earned. The number of required tokens may be increased as the student is more successful.

- Design data collection procedures. Data can be collected based on the number of successful exchanges or the frequency of the desired behavior.

For example, Elizabeth's problem behavior involves running around the classroom in order to avoid circle time. The team has decided to start Elizabeth on a token system to earn breaks from circle time. They decide that Elizabeth will begin by receiving one token for coming to circle. She can then exchange that token for a picture of the "Break Card" in the classroom. The "Break Card" serves the same function as the problem behavior; she is still able to escape from circle. The classroom staff can now govern when and how Elizabeth is dismissed from circle. As the desired replacement behavior is implemented, the number of tokens needed for a break will increase. The process for implementing the token economy system for Elizabeth is as follows:

1. Identify an appropriate sturdy token board.

2. Identify appropriate tokens such as coins, stars, plastic chips, or stickers. An appropriate token can be very rewarding in itself. Place Velcro® on the back of each token.

3. Determine the reinforcement to be exchanged for the tokens. For Elizabeth the reinforcement is a picture of the "Break Area" where she can go for a short period (one to two minutes) to "escape" from circle time.

4. Begin the token economy with the student earning as few tokens as possible. The team has decided to start Elizabeth with one token.

5. Be consistent in exchanging the tokens for the reinforcement. Elizabeth will receive "Break Area" time whenever she comes to circle time.

6. Gradually increase the number of tokens needed for exchange. For Elizabeth, after a period of success with one token, she will have to earn two tokens before receiving reinforcement. The staff must remember to modify circle time to insure that the first activities are highly rewarding to Elizabeth.

7. As Elizabeth increases her time in circle, the staff will provide reinforcement for the desired behaviors.

Token economies provide an easy to use system for reinforcing desired behaviors while teaching an alternative behavior which meets the desired function for the student. In the case of Elizabeth, the staff can strongly reinforce the student for attending circle time while teaching her an appropriate skill to escape from an undesired activity.

Key Concept: Negative Reinforcement

Elizabeth's story depicts an appropriate use of negative reinforcement to maintain or increase a desired behavior. Negative reinforcement is the brief escape from a difficult task, or circle time, to decrease noncompliance and other problem behaviors. Elizabeth was provided a break from circle in order to shape and maintain appropriate alternative behaviors. Remember, negative reinforcement does not mean punishment or adverse consequences.

Helpful Hint: Token Economy Puzzles

Another way to create a token economy is to create a picture of the high-quality reinforcer that motivates the student. For example, if a student enjoys working on the computer, take a picture of the computer, laminate it and cut it into several pieces. The number of pieces into which the picture is cut is based on how long the student is able to maintain the desired behavior. Initially, the picture is divided into two pieces. After the picture has been divided, put small pieces of Velcro® on the back of each piece. At this time the student is taught that he must earn a piece of the puzzle in order to receive reinforcement. The completed picture of the computer is a visual cue to the student of his success.

Differential Reinforcement

Differential reinforcement of adaptive behaviors is a proactive strategy that focuses on catching the student exhibiting alternative or replacement behaviors. High-quality reinforcement is provided to the student for the absence of the problem behavior and for exhibiting an appropriate alternative behavior.

The classroom staff is trained to reinforce the student when the maladaptive behavior is not being displayed. All staff must continuously observe the classroom and ask themselves: "What behaviors can I immediately reinforce for this student?" Although differential reinforcement does not involve teaching a replacement skill, it does focus on a positive approach to problem behaviors.

Helpful Hint: Reinforcement Challenge

Providing reinforcement may not be a natural act for all staff members in the classroom. It may be helpful to create a classroom staff challenge to increase the amount of reinforcement provided by each team member. Keep a running tally of every reinforcement a staff person provides to a student. A simple piece of masking tape placed on some clothing can be used as the tally sheet. Have each staff member keep track of the amount of reinforcement they provide in one day. Award a special prize to the winner and challenge them to improve the following day.

Guidelines for Implementing Reinforcement Strategies

Both adults and students alike are motivated by a variety of reinforcement strategies. Therefore, using reinforcement is a key element for teaching students with autism. Most typically developing students are reinforced through task completion and teacher praise, but students with autism are not typically reinforced through these internal methods. They require external motivation to maximize their learning and increase adaptive behaviors. School personnel must identify appropriate reinforcers and use them effectively throughout the school day.

Key Concept: Top Ten List for Insuring Appropriate Behaviors

The following is a precise list of the necessary steps for decreasing problem behaviors and increasing appropriate adaptive skills:

1. High-quality reinforcement

2. Social skills training

3. High-quality reinforcement

4. Functional communication training

5. High-quality reinforcement

Remember, high quality reinforcement increases and maintains the desired alternative and replacement behaviors.

Types of Reinforcers

- Edibles

- Tangibles

- Social Praise

- Activities

Caution: Edibles should seldom be used and then only while other reinforcers are developed.

Guidelines for Selecting Reinforcers

Selecting reinforcers for students with autism is a continuous process which changes throughout the school year. Not all students are motivated by the same items. Selecting appropriate high-quality reinforcement involves:

- Observing the student in the classroom,

- Completing a reinforcement survey, and/or

- Interviewing the student or other adults.

The reinforcement interests of some students may be readily apparent while other students require serious investigation. Some students may have little experience playing with certain toys and games and therefore must be taught to enjoy specific items or activities.

According to Leaf and McEachin (1999), there are a few basic tenets for using reinforcement:

- Reinforcers are contingent upon the student's behavior. The student is only reinforced after meeting the criteria for the task or exhibiting the desired behavior.

- Use a variety of reinforcers to avoid satiation. Each student should have a variety of reinforcers that are rotated frequently. If the same reinforcement is used ever y day, it will lose its potential as a change agent.

- Use age-appropriate reinforcers based on the chronological age, NOT on the developmental age. This makes it finding reinforcers more challenging for secondary students, but the goal is to help the student be functional and independent.

- Don't allow free access to strong reinforcers.

- Select reinforcers which can be readily removed from the student's environment and easily manipulated by the staff.

- Pair high-quality reinforcers with praise to further develop more natural reinforcement. The goal of reinforcement is to reinforce through social interaction with the adult.

For a further discussion of reinforcement selection and implementation, refer to *A Work in Progress* (Leaf & McEachin, 1999).

 Key Concept: Avoid Bribery

Reinforcement is always contingent upon the student's completion of a task or of his exhibiting a desired behavior. Therefore reinforcement is NEVER to be used as bribery. For example, reinforcement would not be provided to a student in the middle of a tantrum. Nor would a student receive a high-quality reinforcer to entice him into working. Bribery teaches the student that he does not have to comply in order to achieve the desired outcome.

Reinforcement Schedules

Reinforcement is provided to the student after the student has met the predetermined criteria for a task or has exhibited a desirable behavior. The rate of reinforcement will be determined based on the task and the individual skills of the student. A reinforcement schedule will assist the staff in determining the appropriate timing for reinforcement. There are several options for a reinforcement schedule:

1. Continuous and Immediate

When first teaching a new skill or desired behavior, reinforcement will be immediate and continuous. This immediate and continuous reinforcement will insure repetition of the desired behavior.

2. Intermittent

As the student progresses with a newly acquired skill or behavior, the reinforcement schedule will be thinned and become more intermittent. An intermittent schedule is like a slot machine: The student may receive the pay-off at different intervals, but the student does not know when the pay-off will occur.

3. Delayed

Delayed reinforcement is used in a token economy system where the tokens are earned and can be exchanged for the reinforcement at a later time. Delayed reinforcement should be systematically scheduled to increase the desired behavior. Inconsistencies with delayed reinforcement increase student frustration and trigger problem behaviors.

4. Provided within the Natural Setting

The goal of reinforcement is to help the student become naturally self-motivating. Ultimately, the student will be reinforced through the completion of the task and naturally occurring consequence. For example, when typically developing students complete all assigned work, they may be allowed to go out for recess and achieve passing grades.

Helpful Hint: Reinforcement Hierarchy

Include a written list of the top ten student reinforcement items as part of the Student Profile. Simply brainstorm all of the reinforcement items from your observation and assessment. List them in order from most powerful to least powerful for increasing or maintaining the desired behaviors. Review the list once or twice a month to make additions and deletions.

Environmental Modifications

Although teaching replacement skills to the student is a daily activity and an integral part of the behavior intervention plan, the classroom staff must also address environmental modifications. To adequately evaluate the environment, the staff can begin by completing the Classroom Inventory from Chapter One. The Classroom Inventory provides general guidance in preparing and designing an effective environment. This simple checklist will insure that the basic principles for the classroom are being addressed.

After completing the inventory the teacher must review the needs of each student. Although the overall classroom may be arranged appropriately, some students will have specific needs that must be addressed. Additional modifications, tailored where possible to the specific needs of each student, will help ensure on-task behavior and increased independence. Specific modifications for the individualized behavior plan may include:

Level of Support:

The student may need more adult assistance to learn a new skill.

Time:

The student may require more or less time to complete an assigned task. Some students may need more breaks in their schedule.

Level of Difficulty:

Be sure to create a curriculum that is neither too easy nor too difficult. Unchallenging repetitive tasks create boredom for the student and will likely increase maladaptive behaviors.

Key Concept: Do Not Support Rigidity

Although great care is taken to modify the environment and curriculum to support the student, it is important not to support a student's tendency to sameness and repetition. In other words, help the student through high-quality reinforcement, to tolerate new classroom arrangements and a variety of activities. Also teach stress reduction skills for students who are frustrated with change.

School personnel can greatly increase the use of replacement skills and adaptive behaviors by controlling distracting ecological stimuli. Addressing environmental modifications is a proactive strategy that can have a very positive effect on student outcomes.

Compliance Training

Complying with teacher directions is one area where many students with autism have difficulty. School personnel often report students who are consistently noncompliant. In other words, "I just can't get him to do anything."

Compliance training is used to teach the student to comply with requests by providing him with reinforcement upon compliance with the request. Compliance training also increases opportunities to teach replacement skills. The higher the incidence of compliance, the more likely the student will follow instructions for learning a new skill. There are a few simple steps for implementing compliance training:

Step 1: Reduce The Number Of Instructions

For students who are extremely noncompliant, the first step in compliance training is to reduce the number of instructions. Staff members should not demand compliance, but should instead focus on those behaviors with which the student will comply. All other demands or instructions should be minimized. For example, if the student enjoys snack time and lunch, the majority of demands will be to "eat your lunch" or "have another bite."

Step 2: High-Quality Reinforcement

The student is reinforced immediately for all compliance. If the student is in the process of sitting down, classroom staff should quickly give the command, "sit down."

The goal is to catch the student exhibiting the desired behavior and quickly provide the instruction. This builds the opportunity for catching the student complying with requests and for providing high-quality reinforcement.

Step 3: Behavioral Momentum

Behavioral momentum, or the sequence of instructions, is another strategy for obtaining compliance with teacher requests. The sequence of instructional demands can greatly influence the probability of compliance. This technique requires that the staff give the student several simple, high-probability requests before making lower-probability requests. Sandwich the more challenging requests between demands that are easy for the student.

For example, if a student is able and willing to comply with such requests as "clap your hands", "touch your nose", and "close the door", the teacher would then give a more challenging demand of "sit down." The student is more likely to comply with the last request, "sit down", after successfully following the first three commands.

Step 4: Introduce New Demands Slowly And With Visual Supports.

Be careful not to overwhelm the student with too many instructions or requests. Keep the demands simple and use a visual cue which depicts the desired behavior to support the request. For example, if the request is for the student to "sit down", the visual cue would show a student sitting in a chair. The visual prompt is shown to the student at the time the command is given.

The staff may also model a visual prompt at the time of the command. If the teacher wants the student to "sit down," the teacher should model the desired behavior while giving the instruction. The teacher can also present a picture of the student sitting while giving the command. The visual cue helps the student process the command and increases the likelihood of compliance.

Step 5: Generalize to New Settings

As student compliance in the classroom increases, the staff introduces demands in other settings. Determine the environment that would most likely support the student's success. For example, if the student has mastered the command "sit down", the staff can expand compliance training to other school settings. Consider structured environments such as the library or music class. Generalizing compliance training across settings will insure that the student has adequately mastered the new skill.

Compliance training is an intensive program and is not intended for all students. Moreover, although compliance training can be effectively implemented in an autism program, it is important to remember that it involves only one aspect of the overall program for a student with autism. The multidisciplinary team should determine the exact plan for the program and decide whether compliance training is appropriate for a particular student.

Reactive Programming

Although the focus of teaching students with autism is on proactive programming, it is also essential to develop a reactive program as part of the behavior intervention plan. In a reactive plan, the team determines the steps that will occur after the maladaptive or problem behavior is exhibited. Reactive programming can further decrease the frequency of problem behaviors and may help regain control in a crisis. In a well-designed program to address problem behaviors, reactive procedures will be used minimally, and then only with respect for the student.

There are several strategies available to school personnel to address behaviors after they have occurred. The multidisciplinary team should consider the least intrusive methods for decreasing the likelihood of problem behaviors. Response cost, extinction, and punishment are a few reactive techniques, which may be used in a school setting.

Response Cost

A response cost technique reduces undesirable behavior by removing a reinforcer. Each occurrence of the problem behavior results in the loss of a reinforcement already earned by the student.

Guidelines for Implementing Response Cost System:

- Clearly define the problem behavior that will result in a loss of reinforcement

- Determine if the student can earn reinforcement back after the loss of reinforcement, similar to a token economy system.

- Be sure to impose an immediate loss of reinforcement after the problem behavior is exhibited by the student. If the loss of reinforcement is delayed, the impact on decreasing the problem behavior may be minimized

- A response cost system may call attention to the maladaptive behavior. If the student is seeking attention, the removal of reinforcement may increase the likelihood of the problem behavior.

- Maintain data collection records to insure the positive impact of a response cost system. Daily frequency counts should demonstrate that the system is effective in decreasing the problem behaviors.

- Response cost systems focus on the consequence of a problem behavior and do not teach replacement skills. Therefore, school teams should combine this program with other proactive programs for addressing problem behaviors.

For example, Stephen is highly reinforced by working on the computer. Therefore, the teacher has laminated the eight letters of the word COMPUTER and placed each individual letter on the Stephens's desk. Each time Stephen jumps out of his seat and runs in the classroom, one letter is removed from the word COMPUTER. For every letter that remains at the end of the day, Stephen will receive five minutes of computer time.

Other response cost programs may include point systems or marbles in a jar. The classroom staff should determine the most effective and efficient system for the individual student.

Extinction

Another reactive technique for problem behaviors is extinction. Extinction attempts to reduce the problem behavior by eliminating the reinforcement that maintains the behavior.

Guidelines for Implementing an Extinction Program:

- Extinction can only occur if the staff is able to control the environment of reinforcement to the student.

- Determine the function of the problem behavior. If the function of the behavior is attention, it is imperative to remove all attention from the student.

- The frequency of the problem behavior may increase upon the initiation of the extinction program. The maladaptive behaviors may get worse before they get better while implementing an extinction program.

- Combine extinction procedures with other proactive programs.

- Caution must be taken not to completely ignore self-injurious behaviors and aggression because of the likelihood the behavior will escalate. In some cases, the staff must provide some minimal attention in order to secure the environment for the student and others.

Minimal attention means:

• A calm and neutral voice

• Little or no eye contact

• Minimal physical restraint

For example, Melissa screams and cries upon entering the classroom each morning. The staff has decided to put her on an extinction program. After keeping baseline data on the length and intensity of Melissa's tantrums, the staff begins by removing any reinforcement to Melissa while she is crying. At first, the staff observes that Melissa cries for a longer period of time upon entering the classroom. But after several days her screams and cries begin to diminish. Specific record keeping demonstrates that after two weeks on an extinction program, Melissa enters the classroom quietly.

Ignoring or paying little attention to some problem behaviors can be an effective procedure in a reactive program. Extinction is a planned reactive intervention and should be used only when the function of the behavior is reinforced through attention from others.

Aversives, Punishment, and Time-Out

I do not recommend using or implementing aversive procedures in school settings for students with autism. Aversives can be characterized as intrusive procedures requiring corporal punishment, use of water sprays, performance of exercise, or the deprivation of necessary food and water. Aversives are not effective over time and may cause the student to fear the adult applying the punishment. Even mild forms of punishment such as verbal reprimands and simple restitution should be used cautiously. School personnel must report any aversive treatment to the proper authorities.

Time-out is often referred to as an effective punishment in a reactive program. Time-out is defined as the loss of access to positive reinforcement or time-out from positive reinforcement. A key principle of time-out assumes that the student is reinforced in the current setting. For example, a typically developing student may be removed from the classroom or reinforcing environment, to an isolated area or punishment. Unfortunately, this is not generally the case for students with autism. A student with autism will most likely perceive the time-out area as reinforcing because:

- There are no demands being placed on him.

- The function of his behavior is escape and avoidance.

- He can initiate self-stimulatory behaviors that are highly reinforcing.

- The classroom is stressful and he needs a break.

- Time-out from reinforcement must be carefully planned and used with caution to avoid reinforcing and increasing the problem behavior.

Guidelines for Implementing Time Out Procedures:

- Determine the placement of the time-out area. Be sure to use the least intrusive nonexclusionary placement.

• Follow state and local guidelines for the use of time out procedures. Obtain parent permission prior to implementation.

• Clearly define problem behaviors that will warrant placement in a time out area.

• Determine the length of time out for each student. A period of 2 to 10 minutes is typically adequate.

• Create a classroom environment that is reinforcing to the student.

• Maintain strict records of time out procedures and data of individual student time out. Analyze the data to determine if the time out procedures are decreasing the problem behaviors.

Time out from reinforcement is a reactive program which should be implemented prudently and ethically. As with all reactive programs, time out should be utilized in conjunction with proactive strategies.

Crisis Management

Despite careful planning and the development of proactive programming, school personnel may occasionally be faced with a crisis. Phases of a crisis cycle are:

Phase 1.   Calm; optimal; comfortable level; baseline

Phase 2.   Trigger, provoked

Phase 3.   Irritable; frustrated; demanding; anxious

Phase 4.   Peak, tantrum, hitting, spitting, yelling

Phase 5.   De-escalation

Phase 6.   Recovery

School personnel must be very aware of the phases of a crisis and the specific triggers for each student.

 Helpful Hint: Student Profile: Triggers

Identify a list of triggers for each student. Have the team write a "worst case scenario" for the student. List all environmental and physiological triggers that could initiate problem behaviors. Also, list some specific strategies that would quickly de-escalate the problem. Review triggers and strategies with the team and include in the Student Profile.

Once a trigger has occurred for the student, it is important that appropriate and meaningful strategies be implemented to re-direct the student.

Guidelines for Crisis Intervention Strategies:

- Encourage the student to use previously taught stress management techniques.

- Control your own response to the trigger and reduce signs that you are agitated or stressed. Remain calm.

- If the student has escalated past the initial stages of a crisis cycle, seek assistance from other adults.

• Maintain a safe environment for the student and others in the classroom.

• Provide the student with some quiet time.

• Minimize any talking to the student. If any demands are placed on the student, include a visual cue as a prompt.

• At the first signs of de-escalation, provide the student with a repetitive or low demand task. Try not to let the student completely escape from the work environment so as not to reinforce the disruptive behavior.

• Contact the parent or family. Provide specific details of any crisis and outcomes.

• Maintain a record of all crisis situations and evaluate the effectiveness of the school plan.

 Helpful Hint: Practice, Practice, Practice

Crisis intervention is a serious undertaking and requires multiple opportunities to practice the correct procedures. Because students are not in crisis every day, it is important for the staff to practice their crisis intervention skills. Practice role-playing different crisis scenarios. Have each staff member devise a plan and discuss the steps for intervention.

Conclusion

Managing problem behaviors for students with autism is often a demanding and overwhelming task. Students with autism may exhibit a wide range of problem behaviors from mild forms of self-injury to violence against others. The multidisciplinary team must proactively address problem behaviors and plan for teaching replacement skills. As well as, develop and implement reactive procedures to minimize problem behaviors. A reactive program should occupy only a small portion of the overall behavior plan. An effective behavior program will combine both proactive and reactive strategies in order to make long term and significant outcomes for students with autism.

Chapter Five

Data Collection

Data collection is a key element in teaching students with autism. It provides school district personnel and parents with vital information on the gains made by the student. Reliable data collection must be periodically obtained throughout the classroom for students with autism. Most notably, data collection is a vital component of a legally defensible autism program. Unfortunately, solid data collection methods have been replaced with teacher observations and anecdotal notes. If programs and school personnel are to be accountable, data collection methods must be systematically addressed.

Chapter Five will address the following objectives, so the reader should be able to:

· Understand the necessary guidelines for data collection

· Examine the key components for creating an appropriate data collection form

· Review a variety of data collection forms

· Implement data collection methods addressing problem behaviors

· Identify the steps for data analysis and individualized student planning

Data collection is an on-going process that provides a permanent record of student learning and the acquisition of new skills. Although data collection must be completed regularly for every student, it does not have to be cumbersome. Data collection can include behavior logs, charts for discrete trial instruction, and student products. Teachers may also use video clips to create a portfolio of student achievements and gains. The IEP team determines the appropriate data collection methods for meeting goals and objectives for each student.

Guidelines for Data Collection:

• Data collection must include specific mastery criteria and measurable outcomes.

• It must be individualized for each student.

• Data collection methods may be implemented at various times throughout the school day.

• All staff are responsible for data collection.

• Data collection forms should be included as part of a student profile.

• Create a data collection area in the classroom for easy access.

• Analyze data regularly to determine program effectiveness and student outcomes

Data Collection Forms

Data collection forms may vary from state to state. Contact your local school administrator for data collection forms that may be issued by the school district. If no specific district forms exist, the staff may create their own data collection forms. In general, data collection forms include the following information:

1. Student name

2. Date

3. Goals and objectives

4. List of target behaviors

5. Table or graph to collect information

6. Reinforcement list

7. Materials

8. Adequate space to report types of prompting

9. Comments

Specific forms should be developed to address both instructional data collection and behavioral data collection. The following data collection form may be used for discrete trial instruction.

Daily Data Collection Form

Student Name: Jessica

Objective:

1.   Match Picture - to - Picture of Animals

2.   Expressively label parts of body

3.   Trace alphabet letters JESSICA

4.   Receptively identify triangle and rectangle

5.

(+ = correct) (- = incorrect response) (P = prompted trial)

Date	Obj #	Student Response										%/ Comments
10/2	2	-	p	p	+	+	-	p	+	+	+	50% - on task
10/2	3	p	p	+	-	-	p	+	+			37% hand/hand
10/3	1	+	+	+	-	p	+	+	+	+	+	80% cow/dog
10/3	2	+	+	+								100% eyes and nose
10/3	4	-	p	+	-	p	p	-				upset in p.m.

Reinforcement Procedures:

Flashlight

Yo-Yo

Behavioral Comments/Prompting/Modifications:

Hand over hand prompting to trace name. 10/3 J. did not want to come in

from afternoon recess - noncompliant.

Steps to Completing the Daily Data Collection Form:

1. Fill in Student Name

2. Write current objectives from the IEP

3. List high-quality reinforcement procedures

4. Make several copies of this form to be used throughout the school week

5. Fill in the date and the number of the targeted objective

6. Record student response for trial-by-trial data collection or at the end of each teaching session

 Key Concept: Data Collection: Keep It Short and Simple: KISS

Specific data collection methods do not have to be used after every lesson or activity. Data collection may occur at different intervals throughout the day. Be sure to vary the times and activities when data is being collected in order to cover all domain areas.

Estimated Data Collection Form

Estimated data may be taken periodically while introducing a new skill or maintaining a skill. Estimated data is not intended to replace trial-by-trial data. The following data collection form is appropriate for estimated data:

Estimated Data Sheet

Student Name: _____Larry_____

Activity/Materials: _____Fine Motor - Small O.T. scissors_____

Reinforcement: _____Superman Keychain / Plastic Slinky_____

Objective: Cut 3 circles Independently	Date 9/20	9/21	9/22	9/23		Comments: L. requires small scissors
	Est. 1	2	2	2		
Objective: Trace letters of name	Date 9/21	9/22				Comments: Ready to check for mastery
	Est. 3	3				
Objective: String 5 beads ind.	Date 9/23	9/24	9/27	9/28		Comments: Use large beads
	Est. 2	1	2	2		
Objective:	Date					Comments:
	Est.					
Objective:	Date					Comments:
	Est.					

Estimated Data Criteria:

1 = 0-33% correct

2 = 34-66% correct

3 = 67-100% correct

Steps for Completing the Estimated Data Form:

1. Fill in student name, materials, and reinforcement

2. List current objectives from the IEP

3. Determine the criteria level of each objective

4. Make copies to be used throughout the school week

5. As soon as possible after completion of the lesson, school personnel should measure and record the estimated data for each objective

6. If school personnel have estimated that the student is mastering the objective, trial-by-trial data should be taken to confirm mastery.

Behavioral Data Collection Forms

Another type of data collection form may include a behavior log for targeting the frequency, intensity and duration of problem behaviors. A behavior log would include:

1. Student name

2. Date

3. Target behavior

4. Antecedents

5. Consequences

The following is an example of a behavior log utilized as part of a functional assessment:

Behavior Analysis Log

Student _____ DOB: _____

Target Behavior: _____

Observer: _____

Date	Time	Setting	Antecedent	Behavior	Consequence	Comments

Steps for Completing a Behavior Analysis Log:

1. Fill in Student Name

2. Clearly define the problem behavior

3. List the date and time the behavior has occurred

4. Describe the setting and/or environment

5. Describe the context and what occurs prior to the problem behavior

6. Write an objective description of the behavior.

7. Describe the consequences after the behavior occurs.

8. List any comments from the observer

The purpose of the behavior log is to identify when and where the targeted behavior is occurring and the specific consequences of the behavior. A behavior log and analysis are discussed in Chapter Four as part of a functional assessment.

In addition to the Behavior Analysis Log, school personnel should also measure and record the intensity, duration, and frequency of problem behaviors. The following data collection forms provide the multidisciplinary team with specific information regarding effectiveness of a behavioral intervention program:

Behavioral Data Collection Intensity

Student _____ Nick _____ DOB: _____ 12/13 _____

Target Behavior: _____ Nick scratches other students and adults _____

Observer: _____ Mrs. Butler _____

Date	Time	Setting	Intensity (#)	Comments
9/21	9:30	Classroom	4	Scratched student in circle
9/21	11:30	Lunch	1	Enjoyed lunch
9/21	2:30	Music room	2	Music is loud and students are dancing. Nick is agitated.
9/22	9:30	Classroom	1	Calm working on computer

Steps to Completing the Intensity Form:

1. Fill in Student Name and Date of Birth

2. Clearly define the target behavior

3. Fill in the name of the observer

4. As a team, determine the criteria for identifying the intensity of a behavior for each student. For example: 1 = calm, sitting quietly, compliant; 2 = agitated, trigger, pacing, fidgeting with fingers; 3 = screaming, running in classroom, crying; 4 = physical aggression towards others

5. Identify antecedents or triggers for the target behavior

Behavioral Data Collection Duration

Student ___Devan_____ DOB: __11/18_____

Target Behavior:____Devan tantrums and falls to the floor crying_____

_____

Observer:_____Mr. Patrick_____

Date	Time	Setting	Duration	Comments
10/15	9:00 - 9:18	Hallway	18 Minutes	Devan did not want to get off the bus.
10/18	12:25-12:40	Cafeteria	15 Minutes	Devan would not come in from recess. Required 2 adults to escort back to class.

Steps for Completing the Duration Form:

1. Fill in Student Name and Date of Birth

2. Clearly define the target behavior

3. Fill in the name of the Observer

4. Identify antecedents or triggers to the target behavior

5. Measure and record the elapsed time per episode of the target behavior

Behavioral Data Collection
Frequency/Rate of Behavior

Student _____ Ben _____ DOB: _3/14_____

Target Behavior:____ Ben is self-injurious and hits his head with his fist.____

_____

Observer:____ Ms. Jones _____

Date	Time	Setting	Frequency/Rate	Comments
9/27	11:00 - 11:30	Classroom	7	Ben appeared agitated with new student
10/3	1:15 - 1:45	Classroom	3	Ben was working on computer

Steps to Completing the Frequency Form:

1. Fill in Student Name and Date of Birth

2. Clearly define the target behavior

3. Fill in the name of the Observer

4. Identify antecedents or triggers to the target behavior

5. Begin by recording the frequency of the target behavior. Frequency counts can be taken utilizing a tally mark on piece of masking tape attached to the student's desk or by using a hand counter that can be purchased.

Behavioral data collection methods should be implemented throughout the behavior change process. Baseline data should take place prior to any proactive and reactive programs occur in order to determine the effectiveness of the behavior intervention plan. On-going data collection results in accountability for the multidisciplinary team and a positive outcome for the student.

 Helpful Hint: Data Collection Schedule

Determine a rotating schedule for data collection. Identify specific days and times for collecting data for each student and for each life domain area. For example, Monday, Wednesday, and Friday, might be data collection days for self-help, social, and fine and gross motor skills, while Tuesday and Thursday will be data collection for sensory, cognitive/academics and play. Be sure to rotate the domains each week to ensure quality data collection.

Data Analysis

Effective data collection requires more than just recording student responses and behavior on a form. Practical data analysis is required to insure that overall progress is taking place. The following questions can assist the team in evaluating the effectiveness of the plan:

- Has the student met the objective criteria written in the IEP?

- Are prompts being used? How are prompts being faded?

- Is adequate reinforcement being provided?

- Are the materials interesting and age appropriate?

- Should the criteria be raised or lowered?

- What is the next step for skill acquisition?

Implementing systematic data collection methods provides the staff with the information necessary to plan an appropriate program for students with autism. Data collection also provides valuable information regarding the effectiveness of the program and the impact on student learning

Chapter Six

TEAM:
Together Everyone Achieves More

Teamwork is the most important element in the long-term success of any educational program for students with autism. Indeed, the demands of teaching students with autism can be daunting, even overwhelming, for one person. Sharing responsibilities and decision making is an essential element in educating children with autism. Unfortunately, special education teachers—particularly those in the area of autism—are often isolated from other teachers. According to Fullan (1993):

> *Isolation of teachers limits access to new ideas and better solutions, drives stress inward to fester and accumulate, fails to recognize and praise success, and permits incompetence to exist and persist to the detriment of students, colleagues and the teachers themselves. (p.4)*

Therefore, an effective program for students with autism requires a collaborative, multidisciplinary team approach. This team includes school administrators, paraprofessionals, related service personnel, parents, and licensed teachers. A collaborative work environment can help relieve the pressure and difficult demands of teaching students with autism.

Chapter Six will address the following objectives, so the reader should be able to:

- Review the roles and responsibilities of the school administrator, paraprofessional, related service personnel and parents.

- Identify the importance of networking and building systematic support

- Provide sources for material and references.

Licensed personnel who work directly with students with autism must create a collaborative and supportive work environment.

School Administration

District and school level administrators play an important role in the overall success of a program for students with autism. They are ultimately responsible for developing and implementing a legally defensible program for students with autism spectrum disorders. School administrators must provide leadership, guidance, and support to teachers and support staff. Unless they value and promote teachers who work with students with autism, the effectiveness of the program will be diminished. Special education teachers, whether from self-contained classrooms or inclusive programs, require comparable supervision and leadership as other educators within the building.

Although some school administrators may not feel adequately trained in the area of autism, they have the authority and responsibility to supervise and evaluate special education teachers and support staff. The roles and responsibilities for school administrators are:

- Develop and implement a clear and concise vision

- Provide clearly established standards and guidelines

- Identify and provide opportunities for teachers to work collaboratively in a coordinated effort

- Conduct and implement formative and summative evaluations of licensed teachers and support staff

- Understand the needs of the classroom and supervise the implementation of curriculum and instruction

- Assist and support licensed personnel in the day to day operations of the classroom

School administrators must actively seek out information regarding autism spectrum disorders and appropriate programming. For programs to be effective, the administrator must provide instructional leadership, determine effective instructional methods, implement clear guidelines, and set high standards.

In some schools, there may be minimal administrative support available to teachers who work directly with students with autism. There are several ways for teachers to gain the support of their administrators:

- State clearly the needs of your program. Provide specific examples of how the administrator may assist the classroom teacher.

- Provide the administrator with easy-to-read articles about autism as well as about effective programs. Make a follow-up appointment to discuss the article.

- If you are having personnel issues, create a plan of action to present to the administrator. Give them a few choices for resolving the problem.

- Agree to provide a staff in-service on autism spectrum disorders. Prepare a short overview of autism and a few basic strategies for classroom teachers.

- Invite the school administrator to visit the classroom and provide them with a list of classroom expectancies.

Professionalism and persistence are powerful methods for gaining support of the school administrator. Approaching the school administrator in this way will result in a more supportive and collaborative working relationship.

Paraprofessionals

The paraprofessional plays a key role in any program for students with autism. Paraprofessionals may be used within a self-contained program, or may be hired as a one-on-one assistant in a general education classroom. Given the breadth of responsibilities of a paraprofessional, they are under immense pressure to perform in a variety of settings and with many different teachers. Although the school district may provide some general training in first aid and student confidentiality, many paraprofessionals have little or no experience or specialized training in working with students with autism.

Because of the unusual nature of the disability, and because of the variety of educational placement options available to students with autism, it is impractical to provide an exhaustive list of all the roles and responsibilities of a paraprofessional. Here are a few essential responsibilities:

- Establish an effective and mutually supportive working relationship with the teacher.

- Determine the specific needs of the student and support the student's needs.

- Seek out specific information regarding autism spectrum disorders.

- Build mutual trust and respect with the teacher and other licensed personnel.

- Attend any workshops or conferences provided by the district.

Paraprofessionals are often placed in challenging situations where they must meet not only the demands of the general education teacher, but also the demands of the special education teacher. They are responsible for many facets of the students' education, yet they have little authority over their work environment.

The classroom teacher, however, can improve the working relationship with the paraprofessional in a number of ways:

- Clarify roles and responsibilities early on.

- Develop rapport and trust.

- Be available to communicate problems without judgement.

- Arrange opportunities to meet with the paraprofessional away from students.

- Jointly develop a job description.

- Provide continuous training or short articles about working with students with autism.

- Learn how to give praise and objective feedback.

- Generate classroom strategies and ideas together.

The teacher/paraprofessional relationship is unusual in that the district rarely provides clearly defined roles and responsibilities. The success of the collaborative working relationship is the responsibility of both the licensed teacher and the paraprofessional.

Helpful Hint: Paraprofessional Job Description

To help support paraprofessionals in the classroom, be sure to write a thorough job description and provide a detailed staff schedule Chapter One. These practical documents will both empower the paraprofessional to work independently and increase her self-confidence on the job.

Communication is vital to the success of any demanding and complex working relationship. Paraprofessionals and licensed teachers must identify and maintain a specific time to discuss work issues and student related topics. Without a clearly established meeting schedule, the relationship between the teacher and paraprofessional will become strained and will eventually reduce the overall effectiveness of an autism program.

Teachers and paraprofessionals alike need opportunities for shared problem solving and decision-making.

Key Concept: Communication

A collaborative work environment built on communication and mutual trust will greatly increase the effectiveness of programs for students with autism. Open communication between teachers and the paraprofessionals is the hallmark of an effective working relationship. Honesty and openness increase trust and ultimately support mutual growth and understanding.

Related Service Personnel

It is not unusual for students with autism to receive educational services from four or five different licensed personnel in one school week. These services may include speech and language services, occupational therapy, physical therapy, music therapy, and nursing services.

Related service personnel are generally responsible for identifying and assessing intervention and prevention services for students with disabilities. In addition, related service personnel also have the following responsibilities:

- Collaborate with other licensed personnel.

- Participate in classroom staff meetings.

- Assist the teacher in generalizing new skills across settings.

- Provide information and training to the classroom. teacher and paraprofessional in order to expand services throughout the school day.

- Recognize the importance of providing services within the classroom.

- Work collaboratively with the teacher, paraprofessionals, and other team members.

Related service personnel often have high caseloads and may have little time for developing or supporting a multidisciplinary collaborative team. The classroom teacher can implement several strategies to help related service personnel work collaboratively:

- Develop a staff schedule that includes related service personnel.

- Jointly develop a job description.

- Communicate specific concerns and a plan of action.

- Share articles and inservice training opportunities.

- Include related service personnel in staff meetings.

- Keep related service personnel informed of changes in students' progress.

- Promote active communication techniques.

- Develop mutual trust and respect.

Related service personnel have special knowledge that classroom teachers generally do not have. Promoting and maintaining a good, cooperative relationship provides the teacher with expertise in these areas.

Parents and Families

Parents and families are an integral part of the educational development of their child. They also play an important role on the multidisciplinary team. Parents' primary responsibility is to share with the team the special knowledge, insights, and experiences that only a parent can have regarding their children. Parents give the team a family perspective by:

- Providing detailed historical information about the child.

- Functioning as a member of the team.

- Sharing responsibility for educational outcomes.

- Providing the professional staff with literature regarding autism spectrum disorders.

- Attending multidisciplinary team meetings.

- Forming and maintaining a collaborative working relationship with parents and families requires dedication and commitment from the professional staff.

Licensed personnel can establish a positive collaborative relationship with families of children with autism in a variety of ways:

- Listen to the information provided by the family.

- Share decision making and accountability for outcomes.

- Communicate regularly about the student's progress.

- Provide an opportunity for the parents to share information and train staff.

- Recognize the expertise the family has regarding their child.

Although parents and families are not at school throughout the day, they can provide an important support and encouragement to classroom teachers.

Licensed Teachers

The Keys to Success for Teaching Students with Autism provides numerous strategies and techniques for both classroom teachers and school personnel. One element that is crucial to the overall success of a program is the ability of the team to create and establish a supportive working environment. Providing the highest quality curriculum and methods can not overcome the disadvantages of working in isolation and without adequate training and support. Therefore, it is vital that school personnel actively seek support and assistance.

There are several networking options for teachers in both rural and urban settings:

1. Find a mentor

Many school districts have organized mentor programs for new teachers. If one is not available in your area, request a mentor from the school administrator. Or, informally ask a colleague if they would be willing to be a mentor.

Meet regularly with your mentor and discuss any problems you are experiencing. If you are a veteran teacher, it is still important to have a colleague with whom to share ideas and resources. Look for other teachers who share your teaching style and begin a support group within the building or school district. Be sure to include related service personnel in your group.

2. Attend a conference

Your school district cannot always afford to send you out of state to attend a conference. Instead, look for conferences near your hometown to cut down on expenses. Or, find a conference over the summer and go as a group. If necessary, remind school administrators of the special education law requiring knowledgeable professionals to work with students with autism.

3. Take a class

If you have a local university, look for college classes related to autism and special education. Ask the local university to provide a course in autism during the summer months. Remember that some college classes are offered on-line. Investigate available coursework through distance education.

4. Join an autism group

There are many regional and national autism groups starting up all over the country. Start with your local school district and inquire about such groups. The group may be geared towards parents, but they always appreciate school professionals attending. An autism support group will have suggestions for conferences, classes, and other avenues for networking.

Key Concept: Coming Together, Sharing Together, Working Together, and Succeeding Together

A committed collaborative educational team can overcome obstacles by pulling together and combining their individual strengths in maximizing the potential outcomes for students with autism spectrum disorders.

Conclusion

In conclusion, *Keys to Success for Teaching Students with Autism* has provided an easy to follow guide for school personnel. It is my hope that after reading and implementing the strategies in this book, teachers feel confident in designing and implementing an effective program for the students in their classrooms. A Classroom Inventory and schedule was reviewed in Chapter One in order to assist teachers in building the foundation for their classrooms. Both environmental structures and schedules are key to a successful program.

Many "Helpful Hints" were presented for curriculum development and implementation. Although teachers are trained to focus on the academic subject areas, it is recommended that particular attention be given to the hidden curriculum. The hidden curriculum would include social skills, play skills, and communication. As suggested in Chapter Two, school personnel must also examine the function of the curriculum and age appropriate materials.

Selecting an appropriate method of instruction for students with autism has been a highly debated topic. Chapter Three reviewed a continuum of instructional methods from

Discrete Trial Instruction to Incidental Teaching methods. The multidisciplinary team must consider the individual needs of the student when determining an instructional method. Teachers should be thoroughly trained in each instructional method with a clear understanding of specific implementation strategies.

Self-injurious behaviors, aggression, and emotional outbursts are some of the problem behaviors exhibited by students with autism. Chapter Four provided both proactive and reactive techniques for managing problem behaviors. School personnel must examine a variety of proactive approaches including reinforcement strategies to minimize problem behaviors and teach replacement skills.

Data collection is the cornerstone of an effective and legally defensible program for students with autism. As discussed in Chapter Five, school personnel must maintain data for all students. A variety of data collection methods and forms were also examined in this chapter. Teachers must begin to prioritize data collection and embed it as part of the daily schedule.

Keys to Success for Teaching Students with Autism was written as a practical planning guide for teachers. Teachers can review the strategies and "Helpful Hints" to determine an action plan for their classrooms. After reading this guide, teachers should select one or two specific areas to focus for further training and development. Create an action plan and determine small measurable goals. Teachers should also network with other professionals to gain peer support and share resources. As each goal is reached, be sure to celebrate the daily accomplishments achieved by both staff and students.

References

American Psychiatric Association (1994). *Diagnostic and statistical manual of mental disorders, DSM-IV* (4th ed.). Washington, DC: Author.

Anderson, G. M., & Hoshino, Y. (1997). Neurochemical studies of autism. In D. J. Cohen, & F. R. Volkmar (Eds.), *Handbook of autism and pervasive developmental disorders* (pp. 325-343). New York: John Wiley & Sons.

Autism Society of America. (1999). *What is autism* [Brochure]. Bethesda, MD: Autism Society of America.

Bettelheim, B. (1967). *The empty fortress: Infantile autism and the birth of the self.* New York: The Free Press.

Cohen, D. J., & Volkmar, F. R. (Eds.).(1997). *Handbook of autism and pervasive developmental disorders.* New York: John Wiley & Sons.

Freeman, B. J. (1997). Guidelines for evaluating intervention programs for children with autism. *Journal of Autism and Developmental Disorders*, 27 (6), 641-651.

Frith, U. (1989). *Autism: Explaining the enigma.* Cambridge, MA: Basil Blackwell.

Fullan, M. (1993). *Change Forces: Probing the depths of educational reform*. London: The Falmer Press.

Gilliam, J. (1995). *Gilliam Autism Rating Scale*. Austin, TX: Pro-Ed.

Goodlad, J. I. (1990). *Teachers for our nation's schools*. San Francisco, CA: Jossey-Bass.

Grandin, T., & Scariano, M. M. (1996). *Emergence: Labeled autistic*. New York: Time Warner Books.

Kanner, L. (1943). Autistic disturbances of affective contact. *Nervous Child, 2*, 217-250.

Klin A., & Volkmar, F. R. (1997). Asperger's syndrome. In D. J. Cohen, & F. R. Volkmar (Eds.), *Handbook of autism and pervasive developmental disorders* (pp. 325-343). New York: John Wiley & Sons.

Koegel, R. L., & Koegel, L. K. (Eds.). (1995). *Teaching children with autism: Strategies for initiating positive interactions and improving learning opportunities*. Baltimore: Paul H. Brookes.

Leaf, R., & McEachin (1999). *A work in progress*. New York: DRL Books.

Lord, C., Rutter, M., & Le Couteur, A. (1994). Autism diagnostic interview-revised: A revised version of a diagnostic interview for caregivers of individuals with possible pervasive developmental disorders. *Journal of Autism and Developmental Disorders*, 24, 659-685.

Lord, C., Rutter, M., Goode, S., Heemsberger, J., Jordan, H., Mawhood, L., & Schopler, E. (1989). Autism diagnostic observation schedule: A standardized observation of communicative and social behavior. *Journal of Autism and Developmental Disorders*, 19 (2), 185-212.

McAfee, J. (2002). *Navigating the social world.* Arlington, TX: Future Horizons.

Mesibov, G. B., Adams, L. W., & Klinger, L. G. (1997). *Autism: Understanding the disorder.* New York: Plenum Press.

Myles, B. S., & Simpson, R. L. (1998). *Asperger syndrome: A guide for educators and parents.* Austin, TX: Pro-Ed.

National Research Council (2001). *Educating children with autism.* Committee on Educational Interventions for Children with Autism. Division of Behavioral and Social Sciences and Education. Washington, DC: National Academy Press.

New York State Department of Health (1999). *Clinical practice guidelines: Report of the recommendations for autism/pervasive developmental disorders.* New York State Department of Health.

Rodier, P. M. (2000). The early origins of autism. *Scientific American*, 2, 56-63.

Schopler, E., Reichler, R. J., & Renner, B. R. (1988). *The childhood autism rating scale (CARS).* Los Angeles: Western Psychological Services.

Scott, J., Clark, C., & Brady, M. (2000). *Students with autism: Characteristics and instruction programming.* San Diego, CA: Singular Publishing Group.

Siegel, B. (1997). Coping with the diagnosis of autism. In D. J. Cohen, & F. R. Volkmar (Eds.), *Handbook of autism and pervasive developmental disorders* (pp. 745-766). New York: John Wiley & Sons.

Simpson, R. L. (1995). Children and youth with autism in an age of reform: A perspective on current issues. *Behavioral Disorders,* 21 (1), 7-20.

Simpson, R. L., & Myles, B. (Eds.). (1998). *Educating children and youth with autism: Strategies for effective practice.* Austin, TX: Pro-Ed.

Stone, W. L., & Hogan, K. L. (1993). A structured parent interview for identifying young children with autism. *Journal of Autism and Developmental Disorders,* 23, 639-652.

Surgeon general endorses intensive behavioral intervention for autism. (2000, Spring). *Science in Autism Treatment,* 2 (1).

Towbin, K. E. (1997). Pervasive developmental disorder not otherwise specified. In D. J. Cohen, & F. R. Volkmar (Eds.), *Handbook of autism and pervasive developmental disorders* (pp. 123-147). New York: John Wiley & Sons.

Tsai, L. Y. (1999). Recent neurobiological research in autism. In D. B. Zager (Ed.) *Autism: Identification, education and treatment* (pp. 63-96). Mahwah, NJ: Lawrence Erlbaum Associates.

Volkmar, F. R., Klin, A., & Cohen, D. J. (1997). Diagnosis and classification of autism and related conditions: Consensus and issues. In D. J. Cohen, & F. R. Volkmar (Eds.), *Handbook of autism and pervasive developmental disorders* (pp. 5-40). New York: John Wiley & Sons.

Wing, L. (1981). Asperger's syndrome: A clinical account. *Psychological Medicine*, 11, 115-130.

Appendix A
Classroom Inventory Checklist

The following inventory is an informal checklist to assist school personnel in creating a positive classroom environment. Each guideline should be reviewed and determined appropriate in meeting the needs of the student. Not all guidelines will apply to each setting or classroom.

Visual and physical boundaries defined	❑ Yes	❑ No
Workstations are labeled with picture and word	❑ Yes	❑ No
Classroom is free of clutter	❑ Yes	❑ No
Space provided for small group and 1:1 instruction	❑ Yes	❑ No
Space provided for whole group instruction	❑ Yes	❑ No
Auditory cue is utilized for transitions	❑ Yes	❑ No
Furniture is appropriate size	❑ Yes	❑ No
Furniture placement defines boundaries	❑ Yes	❑ No
Open spaces are minimized	❑ Yes	❑ No
Materials are clean and in good working order	❑ Yes	❑ No
Extra batteries are available	❑ Yes	❑ No
Shelves are clearly labeled	❑ Yes	❑ No
Students return materials to proper location	❑ Yes	❑ No
Thematic units are utilized	❑ Yes	❑ No
Materials are age appropriate	❑ Yes	❑ No
Bulletin boards are linked to theme	❑ Yes	❑ No
Life domains are addressed in the schedule	❑ Yes	❑ No

Quiet space is provided for Break Area   ❑ Yes   ❑ No

Comfortable seating is provided in Break Area   ❑ Yes   ❑ No

Teacher resources are in a secured location   ❑ Yes   ❑ No

Teacher's desk is out of the way   ❑ Yes   ❑ No

Data collection center is clearly marked   ❑ Yes   ❑ No

Data collection center is accessible   ❑ Yes   ❑ No

Carpets are used to filter noise   ❑ Yes   ❑ No

Outside distractions are minimized   ❑ Yes   ❑ No

Safety standards are implemented   ❑ Yes   ❑ No

Doorways are secured   ❑ Yes   ❑ No

Safety plan is written and posted   ❑ Yes   ❑ No

Classroom Schedule is posted and visible   ❑ Yes   ❑ No

Staff training is provided   ❑ Yes   ❑ No

Reinforcement buckets are established and utilized   ❑ Yes   ❑ No

Class schedule is reviewed daily   ❑ Yes   ❑ No

Schedule reflects any changes   ❑ Yes   ❑ No

Individual schedules are developed   ❑ Yes   ❑ No

Schedule is well-rounded with a variety of activities	❑ Yes	❑ No
Staff schedule is developed and posted	❑ Yes	❑ No
Staff schedule depicts all job responsibilities	❑ Yes	❑ No
Related service personnel are included on schedule	❑ Yes	❑ No
Schedule includes a weekly staff meeting	❑ Yes	❑ No
All staff have a written job description	❑ Yes	❑ No
Staff bulletin board is visible	❑ Yes	❑ No

Action Plan

_____

_____

_____

_____

_____

_____

_____

Appendix B
DSM IV

Diagnostic Criteria for Autistic Disorder

A. **A total of six (or more) items from (1), (2), and (3), with at least two from (1), and one each from (2) and (3):**

    (1)   qualitative impairment in social interaction, as manifested by at least two of the following:

        (a)   marked impairment in the use of multiple nonverbal behaviors such as eye-to-eye gaze, facial expression, body postures, and gestures to regulate social interaction

        (b)   failure to develop peer relationships appropriate to developmental level

        (c)   a lack of spontaneous seeking to share enjoyment, interests, or achievements with other people (e.g., by a lack of showing, bringing, or pointing out objects of interest)

        (d)   lack of social or emotional reciprocity

    (2)   qualitative impairments in communication as manifested by at least one of the following:

        (a)   delay in, or total lack of, the development of spoken language (not accompanied by an attempt to compensate through alternative modes of communication such as gesture or mime)

(b)   in individuals with adequate speech, marked impairment in the

ability to initiate or sustain a conversation with others

(c)   stereotyped and repetitive use of language or idiosyncratic

language

(d)   lack of varied, spontaneous make-believe play or social imitative

play appropriate to developmental level

(3)   restricted repetitive and stereotyped patterns of behavior, interests, and

activities, as manifested by at least one of the following:

(a)   encompassing preoccupation with one or more stereotyped and

restricted patterns of interest that is abnormal either in intensity or

focus

(b)   apparently inflexible adherence to specific, nonfunctional routines

or rituals

(c)   stereotyped and repetitive motor mannerisms (e.g., hand or finger

flapping or twisting, or complex whole-body movements)

(d)   persistent preoccupation with parts of objects

B.   Delays or abnormal functioning in at least one of the following areas, with onset prior to age 3 years: (1) social interaction, (2) language as used in social communication, or (3) symbolic or imaginative play.

C.   **The disturbance is not better accounted for by Rett's Disorder or Childhood Disintegrative Disorder.**

Diagnostic criteria for Rett's Disorder

A. All of the following:

      (1)   apparently normal prenatal and perinatal development

      (2)   apparently normal psychomotor development through the first

             5 months after birth

      (3)   normal head circumference at birth

B. Onset of all of the following after the period of normal development

      (1)   deceleration of head growth between ages 5 and 48 months

      (2)   loss of previously acquired purposeful hand skills between ages 5

             and 30 months with the subsequent development of hand

             movements (e.g., hand-wringing or hand washing)

      (3)   loss of social engagement early in the course (although social

             interaction develops later)

      (4)   appearance of poorly coordinated gait or trunk movements

      (5)   severely impaired expressive and receptive language

             with severe psychomotor retardation

Diagnostic criteria for Childhood Disintegrative Disorder

A.   Apparently normal development for at least the first 2 years after birth as manifested by the presence of age-appropriate verbal and nonverbal communication, social relationships, play, and adaptive behavior.

B.   Clinically significant loss of previously acquired skills (before age 10 years) in at least two of the following areas:

   (1)   expressive or receptive language

   (2)   social skills or adaptive behavior

   (3)   bowel or bladder control

   (4)   play

   (5)   motor skills

C.   Abnormalities of functioning in at least two of the following areas:

   (1)   qualitative impairment in social interaction (e.g., impairment in nonverbal behaviors, failure to develop peer relationships, lack of social or emotional reciprocity)

   (2)   qualitative impairments in communication (e.g., delay or lack of spoken language, inability to initiate or sustain a conversation, stereotyped and repetitive use of language, lack of varied make-believe play)

(3)   restricted, repetitive, and stereotyped patterns of behavior, interests,

and activities, including motor stereotypies and mannerisms

D.   The disturbance is not better accounted for by another specific Pervasive

Developmental Disorder or by Schizophrenia.

Diagnostic criteria for Asperger's Syndrome

A.   Qualitative impairment in social interaction, as manifested by at least

two of the following:

(1)   marked impairment in the use of multiple nonverbal behaviors such

as eye-to-eye gaze, facial expression, body postures, and gestures

to regulate social interaction

(2)   failure to develop peer relationships appropriate to developmental

level

(3)   a lack of spontaneous seeking to share enjoyment, interests, or

achievements with other people (e.g., by a lack of showing,

bringing, or pointing out objects of interest to other people)

(4)   lack of social or emotional reciprocity

B.   Restricted repetitive and stereotyped patterns of behavior, interests, and

activities, as manifested by at least one of the following:

(1)   encompassing preoccupation with one or more stereotyped and

restricted patterns of interest that is abnormal either in intensity or

focus

(2)   apparently inflexible adherence to specific, nonfunctional routines

or rituals

(3)   stereotyped and repetitive motor mannerisms (e.g., hand or finger

flapping or twisting, or complex whole-body movements)

(4)   persistent preoccupation with parts of objects

C.   The disturbance causes clinically significant impairment in social,

occupational, or other important areas of functioning.

D.   There is no clinically significant general delay in language (e.g., single

words used by age 2 years, communicative phrases used by age 3 years).

E.   There is no clinically significant delay in cognitive development or in the

development of age-appropriate self-help skills, adaptive behavior (other

than in social interaction), and curiosity about the environment in

childhood.

F.   Criteria are not met for another specific Pervasive Developmental Disorder

or Schizophrenia.

Appendix C
Life Domain Matrix

Life Domain Matrix

Student _____

Date _____

IEP Goals/Life Domain	Daily Schedule										

Appendix D
Data Collection Forms

Behavior Analysis Log

Student _____ DOB: _____

Target Behavior: _____

Observer: _____

Date	Time	Setting	Antecedent	Behavior	Consequence	Comments

Daily Data Collection Form

Student Name:_____

Objective:

1._____

2._____

3._____

4._____

5._____

(+ = correct) (- = incorrect response) (P = prompted trial)

Date	Obj #	Student Response									%/ Comments

Reinforcement Procedures:

_____

_____

Behavioral Comments/Prompting/Modifications:

_____

_____

Estimated Data Sheet

Student Name: _____

Activity/Materials: _____

Reinforcement: _____

Objective:	Date					Comments:
	Est.					
Objective:	Date					Comments:
	Est.					
Objective:	Date					Comments:
	Est.					
Objective:	Date					Comments:
	Est.					
Objective:	Date					Comments:
	Est.					

Estimated Data Criteria:

1 = 0-33% correct

2 = 34-66% correct

3 = 67-100% correct

Behavioral Data Collection Intensity

Student _____

Name:_____ DOB:_____

Target Behavior:_____

Observer:_____

Date	Time	Setting	Intensity (#)	Comments

Steps to Completing the Intensity Form:

1. Fill in Student Name and Date of Birth

2. Clearly define the target behavior

3. Fill in the name of the observer

4. As a team, determine the criteria for identifying the intensity of a behavior for each student. For example: 1 = calm, sitting quietly, compliant; 2 = agitated, trigger, pacing, fidgeting with fingers; 3 = screaming, running in classroom, crying; 4 = physical aggression towards others

5. Identify antecedents or triggers for the target behavior

Behavioral Data Collection Duration

Student _____

Name:_____ DOB:_____

Target Behavior:_____

Observer:_____

Date	Time	Setting	Duration	Comments

Steps for Completing the Duration Form:

1. Fill in Student Name and Date of Birth

2. Clearly define the target behavior

3. Fill in the name of the Observer

4. Identify antecedents or triggers to the target behavior

5. Measure and record the elapsed time per episode of the target behavior

Behavioral Data Collection
Frequency/Rate of Behavior

Student _____

Name:_____ DOB:_____

Target Behavior:_____

Observer:_____

Date	Time	Setting	Frequency/Rate	Comments

Steps to Completing the Frequency Form:

1. Fill in Student Name and Date of Birth

2. Clearly define the target behavior

3. Fill in the name of the Observer

4. Identify antecedents or triggers to the target behavior

5. Begin by recording the frequency of the target behavior. Frequency counts can be taken utilizing a tally mark on piece of masking tape attached to the student's desk or by using a hand counter that can be purchased.

aking one of these will help the person with AS/HFA identify and relieve his or
er own anger or stress.

acticing these simple phrases will help the person with AS/HFA avoid confusion in
cial situations.

y doing this people with AS/HFA can learn to crack the code of "secret language"!

ith this mnemonic people with AS/HFA can learn how to start a
onversation successfully.

ith this mnemonic people with AS/HFA can learn how close to stand or sit, where
look and how to show that they are listing to the other person when they are having
conversation.

tudents with AS/HFA will practice conversation manners by using this "child's toy."

sing this reward hierarchy will "hook the student in" to better behavior.

veryone wants compliments, but people with AS/HFA will need to learn these rules
deliver them appropriately.

alking through conflict resolution-students with AS/HFA can follow these steps to
ork through disagreements.

ublic and private activities are clearly explained with this ordinary shape chart.

I know in general what I need to do, but how do I do it *specifically* . . .

only $49.95

Navigating the Social World

by Jeanette McAfee, M.D.

— Foreword by Tony Attwood —

This important new book offers professionals and parents a thorough and definitive program with forms, exercises and visual guides for students with AS/HFA and related disorders. Ages 9 to adulthood.

Tony Attwood, Ph.D.
August 2001

When Jeanette and Keith's daughter was diagnosed as having high-functioning autism, their long search for an accurate diagnosis was over. However, they began a new search for knowledge on how to help her. They were determined to learn more about AS/HFA and how to provide effective programs for their daughter. They attended workshops and read the research journals and books that describe these conditions, but soon realized that there is remarkably little knowledge on remedial programs. Jeannette began to seek out other people who had worked with individuals with these disorders. She tapped into the experience of a variety of such people, including parents, teachers, speech therapist, occupational therapists, phsychologist and applied behavioral therapists. She combined this knowledge with eleven years of experience working with her own daughter and with her training in pediatrics, and began writing social, behavioral, and abstract thinking skills programs for her daughter. These programs later became the foundation of this book.

It was while presenting a workshop in California that I met Jeanette. Her determination to learn more about AS/HFA, and treatment interventions included moving the whole family to Australia for three months to participate in the programs I was developing in Brisbane. While in Australia, Jeanette studied with me at my autism clinic and with two autism advisory teachers in the Brisbane region. In addition, we spent many hours assessing her daughter's unusual profile of abilities and designing and implementing programs. We generated many new ideas that combined our respective experience. Jeanette subsequently incorporated many of these strategies into *Navigating the Social World*.

This "how to" book is written both for the novice and experienced professional and will be of enormous value to parents, teachers, and therapists. Jeanette has undertaken considerable work in designing handouts, worksheets and tracking forms that provide a structured, logical and progressive approach. There are clear explanations of the relevant issues for each goal and the activities are consistent with the theoretical models of autism and Asperger's Syndrome. After reading this book you can immediately start a program at home or school.

There is a special focus on recognizing and coping with emotions, communication, social understanding, and abstract thinking with practical examples and quotations from individuals with AS/HFA. Jeanette adopts a common sense approach and I strongly recommend this book for parents, teachers, and professionals.

Jeanie McAfee, M.D.
August 2001

When I originally started writing, this book was not even an idea in my mind. I wrote simply to provide a social and emotions program for my then ten-year-old daughter, Rachel. Rachel had just been diagnosed with high-functioning autism (HFA) after years of puzzling physicians, teachers and my husband and me with her unique combination of strengths and special needs. After years of uncertainty about both her diagnosis and how to best help her with the multiple problems she faced, my husband and I reacted to the news of Rachel's HFA diagnosis with relief. We believed we finally would be able to find an appropriate treatment program for her. However, we soon discovered that such a program was not going to be easy to find. Asperger's Syndrome (AS) had only been recognized as a distinct diagnosis under the umbrellas of Pervasive Developmental Disorders (PDD) in the DSM IV in 1994. Thus it was no wonder that little was known about its diagnosis and etiology, and even less about how to treat it. In fact, my husband and I, both physicians, had never heard of either HFA or AS during our medial training. So we were sympathetic when the physicians and psychologist who diagnosed our daughter sent us on our way with the diagnosis, but were unable to suggest specific treatment programs for her. We turned to the next logical place for program options-our local school district-and found that the special education team, including special education teachers and speech and language pathologist, faced the same dilemma. They had little or no knowledge of this new diagnostic category and had had essentially no training in its remediation. Over the last few years we have spoken with many other families and professionals from different parts of the country who have faced the same lack of trained professionals and available programs for children with AS/HFA. It is this need that has motivated me to write *Navigating the Social World*.

Curricula designed specifically to teach social/emotional, abstract thinking, and behavior management skills to individuals with AS/HFA and related disorders are only now beginning to appear. Many of the ideas in this book have been adapted from teaching and counseling methods that have been in existence for years to meet the specific needs of thee students. Other ideas in this text are new. At this point in time most, if not all, programs designed to help individuals with AS/HFA are, of necessity, at the cutting edge of the field. There simply has not been adequate time to develop and test a wide range of treatment approaches in order to ascertain which of them works best. In short, we are still in the research and development phase of treatment for this very complex and often puzzling group of disorders. This is certainly the case with *Navigating the Social World*. For this reason, any input that you, the reader, can give about your experiences using the programs would be greatly appreciated. I hope to use feedback from readers to improve the programs in the future and to provide a forum for sharing ideas. I strongly believe that the more we work together to share ideas and experiences, the better we will be able to help our students, clients, and loved ones with AS/HFA and related disorders to live happier and more productive lives.